BEYOND
COMPETITIVE
ADVANTAGE

BEYOND COMPETITIVE ADVANTAGE

HOW TO SOLVE THE PUZZLE OF

SUSTAINING GROWTH WHILE

CREATING VALUE

TODD ZENGER

HARVARD BUSINESS REVIEW PRESS

Boston, Massachusetts

Library of Congress Cataloging-in-Publication Data
Names: Zenger, Todd R., 1959- author.
Title: Beyond competitive advantage : how to solve the puzzle of
    sustaining growth while creating value / Todd Zenger.
Description: Boston, Massachusetts : Harvard Business Review Press,
    [2016]
Identifiers: LCCN 2015049492 (print) | LCCN 2016004771 (ebook) |
    ISBN 9781633690004 (hardback) | ISBN 9781633690011 ()
Subjects: LCSH: Strategic planning. | Management. | Leadership. |
    BISAC: BUSINESS & ECONOMICS / Strategic Planning. | BUSINESS &
    ECONOMICS / Management. | BUSINESS & ECONOMICS /
    Leadership.
Classification: LCC HD30.28 .Z43 2016 (print) | LCC HD30.28 (ebook) |
    DDC 658.4–dc23
LC record available at http://lccn.loc.gov/2015049492

ISBN: 9781633690004
eISBN: 9781633690011

To Shawn

CONTENTS

PREFACE

As a business school discipline, strategy is remarkably new. By many accounts, its status as a discipline within business schools didn't take hold until after the publication of Michael Porter's books, *Competitive Strategy* in 1980 and *Competitive Advantage* in 1985. These books powerfully translated industrial organization economics into useful tools and logic for managers, and firmly entrenched *competitive advantage* as the strategist's central object. Corporations were to discover and occupy a unique and valuable position that delivered sustained profits beyond that enjoyed by competitors. From these ideas evolved concepts that have shaped pedagogy in strategy courses for decades.

In 1996, I began teaching a course labeled corporate strategy—a course aimed at developing strategic thinking beyond competitive advantage. Rather than the pursuit of position, the course focused on the pursuit of growth and sustained value creation. However, the state of pedagogy on the topic of corporate strategy was poor, largely a string of loosely related topics with scattered guidance and no coherent central message. Unfortunately, it largely remains so. Instructors on the topic have something to say about leveraging capabilities and seeking relatedness. They have some logic to provide regarding vertical integration decisions, and some rather unrelated guidance to offer for managing investments, pursuing acquisitions, and composing organization design. However, unlike the well-packaged and tightly integrated logic of a business strategy course, guidance on corporate strategy remains scattered and fragmented.

Moreover, I quickly recognized that our challenges in teaching corporate strategy were not lost on executives who tried to absorb it. While the topic of corporate strategy resonated, as executives viewed sustaining value-creating growth as their primary challenge, they too were frustrated with the rather à la carte approach that guidance on corporate strategy offered.

This book emerged out of this intense dissatisfaction with the guidance that business professors and thought leaders have to offer about how to sustain value creation. Relative to most popular business books on the topic, this book takes a distinctly different tack. The book does not distill lessons from a set of successful firms (though the book provides abundant illustrations). Instead, the book targets the thoughtful and aspiring strategist with an approach reminiscent of Porter's translation of industrial organization economics. While Porter distilled and synthesized logically sound and well-tested research into a compelling framework and approach, he offered no simple answers. Instead, he highlighted critical questions and trade-offs, and introduced a structured approach to strategic thinking. As I noted, the result has powerfully shaped the rhetoric and reasoning that managers deploy in the pursuit of competitive advantage.

My aim in this book is to translate, illuminate, and synthesize a very different body of academic work, often labeled organizational economics, to answer a different set of questions, surrounding the path to sustained value creation through ongoing efforts to organize and arrange assets and activities. Fortunately, there is an abundance of relevant literature, some of it my own, but much the work of others, including Nobel Prize–winning economists. But surprisingly, almost all of it remains outside the lexicon and logic that managers routinely deploy in evaluating and developing patterns of growth. My contribution is to provide a synthesis and translation, illuminating the power of a more common logic and language, with the aim of providing the thoughtful or aspiring strategist with an enhanced capacity to generate and sustain effective growth strategies.

A central message of the book is that a strategist seeking to sustain value creation needs more than a map to a position. The strategist needs a corporate theory of value creation, something that provides ongoing guidance to the selection of positions and a vast array of strategic actions. In much the same way that a scientist's insightful theory reveals promising experiments to conduct, a well-crafted corporate theory reveals a succession of promising strategic experiments—a succession of strategies and strategic choices. Better corporate theories reveal better strategies—strategies with a higher probability of success. Moreover, a well-crafted corporate theory elevates the strategist's task of sustained value creation from a series of à la carte decisions about acquisitions, investments, design, financing, integration decisions, and leadership, each guided by rather fragmented logic, to a more coherent set of choices guided by a synthetic logic. The book illuminates the attributes of an effective corporate theory, connects corporate theory to valuable logic in organization economics, and highlights a corporate theory's role in sustaining value creation. My hope is that upon completion of the book, you will have a clear understanding of strategic thinking that can move your organization beyond competitive advantage and toward sustained value creation.

Introduction

The basic principles of business-level strategy as taught in business schools and practiced in companies are simple: discover, target, and then craft attractive market positions that deliver sustained advantage in competitive markets. Firms achieve these positions as they configure and arrange resources and activities in ways that yield either unique value to customers or common value at uniquely low cost. This concept of strategy as position remains a central concept to business school curricula across the globe. Valuable positions, protected from imitation or appropriation by others, provide sustained profit streams.

The problem with this view of strategy is that investors reward companies only once for discovering, occupying, and defending a valuable market position. Once the achievement of that position is recognized and valued, investors turn and ask for more, and more requires successfully delivering either unexpected extensions of the current advantage or—more desirable—creating new advantages altogether. Gratitude for past performance is not part of the valuation equation. Indeed, equity markets are filled with firms that command powerful market positions but possess sluggish stock prices. These organizations certainly deserve praise for strategic foresight in crafting their advantage and merit praise for defending them. Unfortunately, investors are not interested in history. For managers, therefore, the goal is not a stable, cash-generating position, but a path to sustained new and profitable growth.

To help managers toward that goal, this book presents the concept of the *corporate theory* as a means of providing managers and executives with a framework for thinking beyond competitive advantage as they negotiate a changing and challenging environment in search of sustained value creation. As with a scientific theory, the object of a corporate theory is to maximize the probability of selecting valuable paths while minimizing costly mistakes. A good corporate theory thus provides a compass for those at the strategic helm and will, from time to time at least, help them beat the expectations baked into their current share prices or, in the case of privately held firms, investors' valuations.

A corporate theory is not an abstract academic construct set about with obscure equations and language. It is rather a narrative, an explanation, or even an image that reveals how a particular company can accumulate value or compose competitive advantages over time. Fortunately, we as humans are actually predisposed to composing theories, possessing in the words of philosopher Charles Sanders Peirce,

" . . . a natural adaptation to [imagine] correct theories of some kinds."[1] Of course, these theories are not always good or correct, but more will flow—and some will be good.

Let me begin by exploring in more detail why a concept such as the corporate theory is needed.

The Limits of Competitive Advantage

Few would dispute that the original business strategies of Dell Computer, Walmart, and Southwest Airlines were remarkable in composition. Each of these companies achieved a strong position of advantage in a very competitive industry. Yet over the most recent decade and a half, each has battled to discover and develop new sources of value, or at least sources not already anticipated or expected by investors. A brief look at these companies and their struggles to create value illustrates the difficult challenge of sustaining value creation.

Walmart's early success reflects an initial decision to focus on small towns and create a regionally dense network of stores. Within these small towns, Walmart enjoyed not only its unique presence as the only discount retailer, but also efficient logistics stemming from high store density within each region. Complementary investments in advertising, pricing, and information technology all supported a position of low cost and stores stocked to suit local tastes. However, despite Walmart's strong position and successful strategic rollout, its equity price has seen little growth since 1999. After hitting $69 per share in December of that year, the stock price fluctuated between the mid-$40s and high $50s for the next thirteen years, despite continued revenue growth. Only in recent years has its share price rebounded to match its 1999 level. Its ongoing successful strategy was long ago anticipated by investors and baked into the current share price. For its market value to rise significantly, Walmart needs to reveal a source of new, unexpected growth, such as the capacity to profitably expand at large scale in developing global regions.

Southwest's story is similar. For several decades, it has maintained a profitable and well-crafted strategic position. Like Walmart, Southwest has assembled highly complementary activities, quite different from its competitor airlines, that have delivered a distinct cost advantage—a position that competitors have been unable to replicate. Nonetheless, Southwest's share price was stagnant for a decade. After the price per share broke through $22 in December 2000, it took until 2014 for the value to approach that number again. More recently, declining fuel prices have elevated the entire industry's market valuations, but for much of the previous fifteen years the market awaited the unveiling of a novel and unexpected source of growth.

The positioning advantage that Dell created in the 1990s has become the stuff of legends. Through a unique set of activity choices, Dell dramatically reduced both its parts and its finished goods inventories—which were depreciating at 5 percent a month. By cutting these massive expenses, Dell enjoyed a sustained cost advantage that competitors found nearly impossible to replicate and that drove a meteoric rise in Dell's market capitalization.

Yet Michael Dell would also learn the painful lesson of investors' unrelenting demand for new and unexpected sources of growth. Adding to the pain was a public pronouncement about what he viewed as Apple Computer's dismal future. At an international IT convention in 1996, a reporter asked Michael Dell what he would do if he were running his struggling competitor Apple. He boldly pronounced that he would shut Apple down and redistribute its assets. A decade of stagnation in Dell's share price soon followed. Apple, meanwhile experienced a meteoric rise in value as it transformed itself from a computer manufacturer into a giant across three industries: consumer electronics, music retailing, and mobile phones.

Each of these anecdotes illustrates one critical point. Sustaining competitive advantage—the commonly understood outcome of brilliant business strategy—does not sustain value creation, the ultimate goal for most firms and their shareholders. Walmart, Southwest, and Dell all struggled to move beyond their initial, enormously valuable position to discover another—and, by this logic, another to follow. This need to sustain value creation is what makes the strategist's job so remarkably difficult. While the rare firm crafts an effective business strategy that preserves a valuable position, only the exceptionally rare sustains value creation. A brilliant business strategy is tremendously difficult to repeat.

What's more, the powerful competitive advantage enjoyed by firms like Walmart, Dell, and Southwest often ends up functioning as a straitjacket. As Michael Porter points out, "[E]fforts to grow blur uniqueness, create compromises, reduce fit, and ultimately undermine competitive advantage. In fact, the growth imperative is hazardous to strategy."[2] Quite simply, therefore, the positioning concept—the backbone of what we commonly teach in strategy—not only provides little guidance about how to find new sources of value creation, but the logic itself may discourage growth that might in any way move a firm away from its current strategic position. So while the positioning logic recognizes the manager's dilemma, it offers no real strategic guidance beyond "Dig in."

The Tyranny of Growth Expectations

Digging in, however, does not cut it in the capital markets. Investors want newly discovered, unexpected value. Moreover, this new value must be of compounding magnitude—tomorrow's positive surprise must be bigger in dollar magnitude than yesterday's. Imagine assuming the reins of GE from Jack Welch in September 2001. Over the previous two decades, GE had generated a fifty-one-fold increase in value for shareholders. The future growth rate implicitly assumed by the market was exceptionally high. The conclusion to be drawn from these daunting expectations was clear: taking over from Jack Welch was a bad gig.

UCLA's Richard Rumelt provides a clever illustration of role of expectations in defining the CEO's plight. He suggests that our approach to evaluating CEOs is analogous to a teacher grading students' final exams based on performance expectations determined at the onset of the course.[3] Thus, an 80 percent score on the final exam from a student expected to receive 95 percent merits a "D," while the same 80 percent score from a student expected to receive 70 percent merits an "A+." Sounds absurd, but as Rumelt notes, this is precisely how we evaluate CEO performance.[4] Past performance establishes expectations that define present value. When high, these expectations render today's task of uncovering improvement substantially more difficult.

Best-Selling Business Books and Future Performance

To make matters worse, past success in sustaining value creation is no guide to future performance. Consider most of the firms extolled in best-selling business books of the "excellent companies" genre. These books typically select a number of firms that have been highly successful at creating shareholder value (or have delivered sustained financial performance by some other measure) and then offer explanations for their historic success.

In 1982, for example, two McKinsey consultants, Tom Peters and Robert Waterman, published *In Search of Excellence*, which looked at forty-three firms that were highly successful value creators in the 1960s and 1970s. Peters and Waterman documented what the firms had in common.[5] While many of the principles and practices they described have survived in the marketplace of ideas, the performance of the firms post-publication clearly suggests that sustaining value creation overtaxes the capacities of even the historically most successful management teams. By 1984—less than three years after the book first appeared—the eroding performance of these "excellent companies" was quite evident to even the popular press. In that same year, *Business Week* reported that fully one-third of the firms had experienced significant financial troubles.[6]

In 1994, Jim Collins and Jerry Porras identified another set of successful firms and generated another blockbuster book, *Built to Last.*[7] Using a similar format, they compared eighteen long-term surviving firms identified as "visionary" by CEOs to a matched sample of similarly long-surviving, but less visionary firms. While the "visionary" companies' historic performance at the time of publication was spectacular, their post-publication performance was quite ordinary, matching closely the Dow Jones Industrial Average. In 2001, Collins's sequel, *Good to Great,* similarly documented eleven companies that significantly outperformed the market over fifteen years.[8] Between the time of the book's publication in 2001 and 2007 (just before the market crash), three of the eleven had experienced reductions in market value, one was essentially flat, and one had been acquired. Again, the overall performance of a portfolio of these eleven firms essentially paralleled the Dow Jones Industrial Average.

The above findings are all consistent with a recent McKinsey study that found that nearly half of the firms that had grown at rates above 15 percent between 1994 and 1997, were growing at rates below 5 percent ten years later.[9] While these observations of their subsequent difficulties don't necessarily invalidate explanations for these firms' historic success, they do vividly illustrate that even the historically best find sustained value creation tremendously difficult.

Is Strategy Bunkum?

Unsurprisingly, perhaps, skepticism of competitive advantage, as strategy's central concept, is growing. To begin with, many critics point out that competitive advantage is increasingly temporary in nature, given the accelerating pace of change in business, technology, and society. All too often, new entrants disrupt established strongholds with entirely different models at considerably lower cost. In this environment, which characterizes what many see as the business landscape of the future, competitive advantage seems to be an outdated idea. Instead, focus is shifting to developing more dynamic strategies that allow corporations to effectively navigate these volatile, uncertain, and highly competitive environments.

Yet the "dynamic strategy" school of thought suffers from its own problem: some adherents end up arguing (implicitly, at least) that strategy is all about reacting quickly to technology-enabled shifts in consumer tastes. But strategy cannot be reduced to reaction. Inherent in the very notion of strategy is the idea of direction; firms create strategies because they see themselves as embarked on a journey. Simply sailing the boat out and seeing where the weather takes you is not a way to run a company. To motivate people to work for your company and convince investors to put their capital into your ideas, you have to offer them more than a philosophy of reaction. Developing a capacity to respond in an uncertain environment is certainly critical for survival—critical to replacing a dissolving position—but it is not a substitute for strategy

The other main post–competitive advantage approach to strategy suffers from a similar problem. In a world of constant change, so the argument goes, companies must experiment their way to success. The sequence is as follows: run experiments, get feedback, and then pivot accordingly. Here fast doing, not thinking, is the coin of the realm. Like the capacity to respond, running experiments is central to sustaining value creation, but the probability that a more or less randomly selected set of them will uncover substantive new value is very small indeed. For experimentation to have a high probability of generating real value, a guiding logic must help the manager choose the right experiments. The world of scientific discovery is instructive in this respect. It is seldom the pace or number of experiments that fuels great scientific discovery, but rather the quality of the theories that guide their selection. Think of space exploration: most of space is empty, so setting about on a random exploratory path is unlikely to discover much of anything, at least not quickly. Moreover, in general, experiments are extraordinarily costly to undertake. Simply letting a thousand flowers bloom will likely exhaust funds long before any valuable discovery is made.

In this respect, the corporate world is no different. Effective experiments test theories, and effective strategic experimentation requires direction just as much as scientific experimentation. This is what a corporate theory provides.

Defining the Concept

So what exactly is a corporate theory? I define it as *a logic that managers repeatedly use to identify from among a vast array of possible asset, activity, and resource combinations those complementary bundles that are likely to be value creating for the firm.* In this sense, it is a predictive framework that generates hypotheses about how alternative strategic actions will create value in envisioned future states of the world. An effective corporate theory permits powerful thought experiments and counterfactual reasoning, enabling a corporation to predict strategic outcomes long before costly investments are undertaken.

A corporate theory may define a set of customer problems that the corporation perceives it is advantaged in solving (think Apple), thereby directing the ongoing assembly of assets and activities required to pursue them. It may define a domain of external assets the firm perceives it is uniquely advantaged in improving (think Danaher as it evaluates acquisitions to pursue), thereby permitting the discovery of bargain prices. It may illuminate valuable investments unseen by others (think Monsanto in entering agricultural biotechnology), allowing sustained valuable investment long before others recognize that value. Moreover, it may reveal complementarities among the identified assets to acquire, problems to solve, or investments to make where the value of pursuing one is greatly enhanced by pursuing the others. In this sense, a corporate theory is not really *a* strategy per se, at least not in the sense of an articulated position or competitive advantage. Rather, it is a *guide to the selection of strategies*, a meta-strategy of sorts—a strategy for strategies.

While the quality of a corporate theory is revealed in the strategic outcomes it generates, valuable corporate theories are necessarily unique, permitting corporations to pursue paths others don't see or cannot access. Corporate theories provide managers with enhanced vision or perspective in three key ways. First, they provide *foresight* concerning the future evolution of the relevant industries, technologies, and customer tastes. Second, they provide *insight* regarding sustainably unique assets, resources, and activities possessed by the firm. Third, they provide *cross-sight*—a recognition of patterns of complementarity between assets, activities, and resources both within and outside the firm. Disney's remarkable corporate theory and how it reflects each of these sights will be discussed in detail in chapter 1, but to anchor initial thinking, let me articulate Disney's theory in simple words:

> Disney believes that noble, engaging characters composed in visual fantasy worlds, largely through animation, will have vast and enduring appeal to children and

adults alike [foresight], and that it will sustain
value-creating growth by developing an unrivaled
capability in family-friendly animated and live-action
films [insight] and then assembling other entertainment assets that both support and draw value from the
characters and images developed within these films
[cross-sight].

Today, Disney's theory is quite widely understood, but in the
1940s and 1950s, it was unique and few people had figured
it out. More importantly, even when people did figure it out,
attempts to replicate it successfully have been hindered by
an inability to replicate the unique assets that support it. The
theory has fueled Disney's strategic experiments for seventy-
plus years. Some strategic experiments have failed, but most
have worked and have provided a succession of positive
surprises to the market.

What's Coming

In the following pages, I will explore the concept and the
reality of the corporate theory, highlighting its importance
in efforts to sustain value creation and exploring its central
role in guiding a wide range of strategic choices. The book is
divided into three parts.

In part one, I discuss the creation of the corporate theory. Chapter 1 illustrates the concept and discusses fully the
central attributes of an effective corporate theory. Chapter 2

focuses on the critical importance of uniqueness in composing a corporate theory and the role of uniqueness in driving
sustained value creation. Chapter 3 examines the paradoxi-
cal conclusion that the most valuable corporate theories are
also the most difficult to fund and finance. It also illuminates
solutions to this dilemma.

Part two looks at the challenges of putting together the
combinations of assets and resources that the theory reveals
as value generating. Chapter 4 highlights the logic of make-
or-buy decisions and illuminates the role that a corporate
theory plays in these choices. Chapter 5 then explores the
role that corporate theory plays in selecting optimal ways to
structure relationships with assets, activities, and partners
that optimally lie outside the firm.

Part three turns to the internal organization and leadership of the firm. In chapter 6, I explore organization design's
central role in sustaining value creation, highlighting in
particular the need to dynamically organize according to
a corporate theory. Chapter 7 highlights the central role of
strategic leaders throughout organizations of all sizes who
can compose and test theories of value creation.

By the end of this book, you should have a good idea of
what a corporate theory looks like; an understanding of its
implications for how the firm builds, acquires, and accesses
the assets and resources that sustain value creation; and
a sense of how to approach the organization and leadership challenges involved in putting corporate theories
into practice. While the book highlights the elements of a
valuable corporate theory, what it will not do is explain the

process whereby you should construct your own corporate theory. These processes are very context-specific, even person-specific. Nevertheless, knowing what distinguishes a good theory from a bad one and knowing how a theory shapes a host of implementation decisions is an important place to start.

PART ONE

Creating the Corporate Theory

CHAPTER 1

Foresight, Insight, and Cross-Sight

Value creation in all domains, from product development to strategy, involves a process of creatively recombining existing elements in novel ways.[1] James Burke, author of the PBS series *Connections*, which documents the origins of great discoveries, noted that: " . . . at no time did an invention come out of thin air into somebody's head . . . You just had to put a number of bits and pieces that were already there, together, in the right way."[2] Steve Jobs similarly characterized the design process as "keeping five thousand things in your brain . . . and fitting them all together . . . in new and different ways to get what you want."[3]

The corporate strategist's task is no different. It is to assemble available assets, capabilities, and activities in new ways in search of competitive advantage for the firm. But more importantly, the corporate strategist's task is to do this successfully over and over again. This is like an almost-blind explorer navigating a rugged, mountainous landscape in constant search for a higher peak. Since she cannot clearly see the terrain, she must develop some theory of what she will find, drawing from available knowledge and past experience. Then, by conducting strategic experiments, which in the corporate world amounts to assembling assets and activities, she gains a clearer vision of some limited portion of this topography.

Strategic experiments can be costly and time-consuming. They may require several years to assemble, and often involve highly specialized and largely irreversible investments. Consequently, engaging in a purely random, experimental search for increased value is unacceptable. That's why good strategists compose theories of how to navigate this terrain. Like a scientist's theory, the strategist's theory generates hypotheses that guide actions.[4] Theories define expectations about causal relationships: *If the world functions according to my theory, then this action will generate the following outcome.* They are dynamic and are updated based on evidence or feedback received. They permit low-cost thought experiments, thereby minimizing expensive, misguided investments.

Just as academic theories enable scientists to generate breakthrough knowledge, corporate theories give birth to value-creating strategic actions. More-effective managers compose more-accurate and powerful theories—theories that open a vista of valuable experiments—a pathway toward value and a domain of value creating actions. The history of

The Walt Disney Company provides an exceptional illustration of a brilliant corporate theory.

The Greatest Theory Ever Told

Walt and Roy Disney founded Walt Disney Productions in 1923. It quickly became the world's premier animator, as the brothers, chiefly Walt, made a series of important advances in the art, technology, and practice of animation. But it was in the late 1940s and early 1950s that Walt came up with what was arguably his greatest creation—a corporate theory for the company —a clearly defined picture of how it would sustain value creation in the entertainment industry.

Walt Disney's theory defined the firm's composition, illuminated the relationships between the individual assets and resources that comprised it, and revealed paths for current and future investment. He captured this theory in the remarkable image shown in figure 1-1, which was retrieved from the Walt Disney Archives. It depicts a range of entertainment-related assets—book publishing, music, magazine publishing, comic books, theme parks, and consumer products—surrounding a core activity in film production, particularly animated film. The archives contain several versions of this theory, which evolved over time.

The drawing also describes a massive web of synergistic connections between these distinct businesses and assets, many linking directly to the central animated film asset. Comic strips "promote films," and films "feed material to"

FIGURE 1-1

Walt Disney's theory of value creation in entertainment

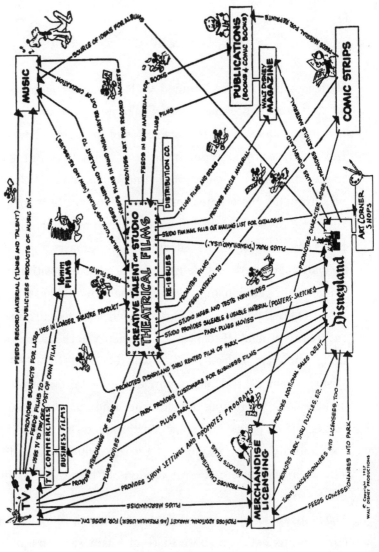

comic strips. The theme park, Disneyland, "plug[s] movies," and film "plug[s] [the] park." TV "publicize[s] products of the music division," and the film division "feeds tunes and talent to" the music division. This picture is more than just an asset description. It visualizes how these assets can be tightly linked to one another as complements, so that the value of one activity or asset is enhanced by the presence of another. As noted in the introduction, Walt Disney's theory might be summed up as follows:

> Disney believes that noble, engaging characters composed in visual fantasy worlds, largely through animation, will have vast and enduring appeal to children and adults alike, and Disney will sustain value-creating growth by developing an unrivaled capability in family-friendly animated and live-action films and then assembling other entertainment assets that both support and draw value from the characters and images developed within these films.

Walt Disney's theory of value creation contained several key elements. It defined a valuable and unique asset; it identified patterns of complementarity among all assets; and it implicitly revealed an image of the future evolution of the industry. While this theory clearly evolved with time, the core elements never changed. This corporate theory did not merely define a position in the market; rather, it provided a road map for decades of future investments—a trajectory of growth for sustained value creation. The company continued to identify and assemble new products, services, and assets that fit the theory. Ultimately, the success of this theory played out in product market performance as its pursuit garnered either price or cost advantages in product markets. For instance, The Walt Disney Company enjoyed cost advantages in publishing, because it could cheaply export animated images and dialogue from its films; generating a best-selling children's book for Disney cost a fraction of what its competitors would pay for the same type of product. Similarly, thanks in part to its investments in animated films, Disney could charge higher prices in theme parks and still draw tremendous traffic.

In many ways, the power of Walt Disney's theory was most evident in the firm's performance decline following his death. Leadership at The Walt Disney Company first transitioned to Card Walker and then to Ron Miller, Disney's son-in-law and former Los Angeles Rams receiver, whom Walt had persuaded to leave football to join the organization. Surprisingly, within fifteen years of Walt Disney's death, the company seemed to have lost complete sight of his theory, and by the early 1970s, its investments had even shifted away from animated films. In the process, the engine of value creation ground to a halt. Gate receipts at Disneyland flattened. Film revenues sagged. Character licensing fees from consumer products also dropped. The TV show *The Wonderful World of Disney*, for which American families gathered to watch every Sunday in what seemed like a nationwide group embrace, was dropped from network broadcast, then relaunched on Saturday evenings, only to be definitively dropped from the networks with the launch of the company's cable channel. By the late 1970s, the Disney franchise many had grown to love as young children had seemingly disappeared.

So deep was the company's strategic disarray that in 1984, corporate raiders attempted the unthinkable—a hostile acquisition. In the process, they threatened to essentially dismantle Disney. Saul Steinberg, the notorious corporate raider, took a 6 percent ownership position in Disney and quickly moved toward acquiring 25 percent of the company's equity. To fund this takeover, Steinberg proposed to dismantle Disney and lined up outside investors eager to acquire key assets such as its film library and the prime real estate surrounding its theme parks. The capital markets clearly signaled that Steinberg's proposed dismantling was more valuable than The Walt Disney Company on its current path. The board was faced with the choice of maintaining Ron Miller as CEO, selling the assets to Saul Steinberg, or finding new management.

It went for the third option, hiring Michael Eisner, who promptly rediscovered Walt Disney's original theory of how to create value in entertainment. Guided by it, Eisner invested heavily in animated productions, with Jeffrey Katzenberg leading the effort. What followed was a string of hits beginning with *Oliver & Company* and followed by *The Little Mermaid, Beauty and the Beast, Aladdin,* and *The Lion King.* Box office share grew from 4 to 19 percent and its share of the video rental and video sales income jumped from 5.6 to 21 percent.

Eisner also pushed Disney's character licensing aggressively, resulting in an eightfold growth in the operating income of this business between 1984 and 1994. Attendance and margins at the theme parks rose dramatically, requiring more investments in hotels to serve the sevenfold increase in Disney park attendees. Eisner also diversified into new assets and activities, including retail stores, cruise ships, Broadway shows, and live-action films.

Notably, these new investments followed logically from the Disney theory. Broadway shows drew characters and storylines from animated films. Cruise ships adopted characters and adapted entertainment from theme parks and Broadway shows. Retail stores promoted all of Disney's assets, including theme parks, cruises, and extensive lines of character-related merchandise. By essentially dusting off Walt Disney's theory and aggressively pursuing strategic actions consistent with it, Michael Eisner led The Walt Disney Company to phenomenal value creation. Under his leadership, Disney's market capitalization shot up from $1.8 billion in 1984 to $28 billion by 1994.

It was a remarkable run, but it finally ran out of steam. Between 1994 and 2004, the company's cumulative growth in value was a mere 22 percent. What went wrong? It's possible that Disney had simply exhausted all valuable strategic experiments that the theory revealed, and what remained was the pursuit of opportunities and assets unlikely to yield value. Thus, while the move into Broadway shows was strongly complementary with animated films, character licensing, and theme parks, other strategic moves—such as the acquisition of a local Los Angeles TV station or the purchase of the California Angels baseball team—lacked the same synergies. If this were the case, the theory's inability to reveal new sources of value was the direct cause of Disney's stagnant share price and it was time to create a new theory.

The alternative explanation is simply that Disney had again lost its way and had failed to take actions or make investments consistent with its theory. Much like the period following Walt Disney's death, the company's core asset, animation, had atrophied substantially during the latter decade of Eisner's leadership; many blamed his abrasive management style for the loss of key animation talent. Bottom line—the animation group had failed to keep up with technology trends and ownership of the best-in-the-world animation asset had consequently drifted from Disney to Pixar. Although Disney had access to this asset through a contract for five CGI animated films, its value-creation machine was powered by an engine that it did not own. Relations between Disney and Pixar grew increasingly contentious and finally broke down entirely just before Eisner stepped down. Disney's new CEO, Robert Iger, clearly recognized the centrality of animation in the Disney theory and quickly moved to purchase Pixar, spending more than $7 billion dollars. In doing so, he restored Disney's ownership of the unique asset most central to its theory of value creation (I take up discussion of this specific incident in chapter 4).

More interestingly, perhaps, is that Iger identified potentially new core assets that he believed would complement Disney's constellation of capabilities and resources: the superhero franchise of Marvel Comics and the Lucasfilm/ *Star Wars* franchise. Both feature characters very different

27

from the princess-heavy character set that Disney had historically generated and sustained. It remains to be seen whether these assets represent an extension of Walt Disney's original theory of how value creation worked and will broaden the terrain the organization's value-creating machine can cover, or whether these actions will force Disney to modify its theory. But whatever the outcome of the Marvel and Lucas experiments, it is indisputable that Walt Disney's theory of value creation for The Walt Disney Company provided a road map for value-creating growth that endured many decades past his death—a remarkable illustration of the power of theory to carry on the intentions and sustain the success laid down by one brilliant leader.

The Three "Sights" of Strategy

The Disney strategy has all the hallmarks of a powerful corporate theory. It has consistently given senior managers enhanced vision—a tool to repeatedly use in selecting, acquiring, and organizing complementary bundles of assets, activities, and resources. Importantly, Walt Disney's graphic representation was not really a strategy per se, but rather a guide to the *selection of strategies*—a theory that would shape value-creating strategic actions, including acquisitions, investments, and organization design.

As briefly discussed in the introduction, corporate theories provide managers with enhanced vision, sight, or perspective in three key ways, as depicted in figure 1-2. First, they define

FIGURE 1-2

Pillars of corporate theory

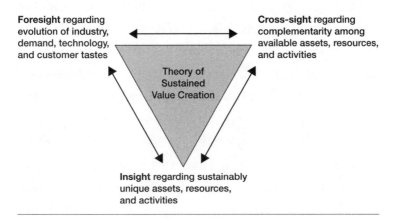

Foresight regarding evolution of industry, demand, technology, and customer tastes

Cross-sight regarding complementarity among available assets, resources, and activities

Theory of Sustained Value Creation

Insight regarding sustainably unique assets, resources, and activities

foresight regarding an industry's evolution in technology and customer demand and tastes. Second, they provide *insight* regarding sustainably unique assets, resources, and activities possessed by the firm. Third, they provide *cross-sight*—revealing patterns of complementarity between assets, activities, and resources both within and outside the firm. Let's look at each of these components in turn.

Foresight

An effective corporate theory articulates beliefs and expectations regarding how an industry will evolve. It may predict future customer tastes or consumer demand. It may foresee the evolutionary trajectory of relevant technologies or forecast the competitive actions of rivals. Ultimately, this foresight offers guidance as to what assets, resources, and activities will prove particularly valuable in predicted future states.

Foresight should be both relatively specific and somewhat different from received wisdom. If it is too generic, it won't identify which options and assets are valuable. If the view it offers is widely shared, then the options and assets revealed will be both expensive to acquire, as others compete for them, and not unique and therefore unable to deliver competitive advantage. Walt Disney's foresight was that family-friendly visual fantasy worlds would have vast appeal and these fantasy worlds could be composed particularly well through animation. While other players dabbled in animation, Disney was the only firm to see its large potential to delight viewers and to invest accordingly.

While theories will differ in the accuracy of their implicit predictions, greater foresight clearly heightens the expected value from the strategic experiments that result. Thus, a first litmus test in evaluating a corporate theory is whether it provides foresight concerning the future value of strategic choices.

Insight

Effective corporate theories identify valuable assets, activities, and resources uniquely possessed by the firm. If competing firms own assets identical to yours, they can often replicate your strategic actions with equal or perhaps even more refined capacity, thereby undermining any value inherent in your foresight. An effective corporate theory is therefore company-specific, reflecting a deep understanding of the organization's existing assets and activities. It identifies those that are rare, distinctive, and valuable.[5] Disney's key insight was recognizing the value of the company's early lead and substantial investment in animation and its capacity to create timeless, unique characters that, unlike real actors, required no agents. Here, the litmus test is whether the corporate theory effectively identifies what is valuable within the firm, thus helping to reveal a set of strategic actions that the firm is uniquely suited to pursue.

Cross-Sight

An effective corporate theory illuminates valuable interdependencies between assets, activities, and resources available to the firm, revealing particularly those complementary to the unique assets and capabilities it possesses. As previously noted, it is this search for *complementarity*—a search for settings where the presence of one element enhances the value of others—that defines the path to value creation. The principle applies to all forms of value-seeking design. Thus, inventors' recognition of complementarity between the horse-drawn carriage, the bicycle, and the internal combustion engine ultimately generated the automobile—a recognition that a four-wheeled steerable carriage was more valuable when creatively connected with the gearing technology of the bicycle and the power source of the internal combustion engine.[6]

For Disney, the remarkable cross-sight inherent in its theory prompted a filtered search for any investments and assets (theme parks, books, music, hotels, cruise ships, etc.) that could leverage unique characters created in films, largely animated films. Since the challenge in sustaining value is to repeatedly assemble value-creating combinations of complementary assets, activities, and businesses, the cross-sight revealed in well-crafted theory is critical.[7] Thus, the final litmus test by which to evaluate a corporate theory is how well it reveals information about the value of various combinations of both existing and externally available assets and resources.

When Theory Guides Strategy: Steve Jobs's Theory of Value Creation

These elements of a valuable corporate theory—foresight, insight, and cross-sight—function interactively in providing the manager with strategic vision. Foresight regarding future demand, technology, and consumer tastes highlights domains in which to search for valuable complementary activities, resources, and assets. Clear insights regarding unique assets focus the search for foresight in industry, technology, or consumer evolution and guide cross-sight in looking for that which is complementary to the unique assets possessed. Finally, cross-sight or a clear perspective on valuable complementarities may reveal assets to acquire, develop, or assemble and highlights the domain of needed foresight. The way Steve Jobs's corporate theory shaped Apple provides a brilliant example.

On August 10, 2011, Apple surpassed ExxonMobil to become the world's most valuable corporation—quite a remarkable feat for a company founded in 1976 and essentially left for
dead in 1997. There is no shortage of explanations for Apple's
success over these decades. While credit has correctly fallen
to Steve Jobs, the real source of his genius has largely been
overlooked. Jobs's greatest creation was not a product, plan
or managerial style. Rather, his genius was a thoroughly contrarian theory of value creation in consumer electronics that
any number of industry experts consistently encouraged him
to abandon. While the details of Apple's history are generally
well known, a brief review illustrates the central role that
Jobs's theory played in their success.

This theory has its origins in the early history of the personal computing industry. The Apple II computer, which may
be said to have launched the industry, was introduced in 1977.
Its inner workings were the brainchild of Apple cofounder
Steve Wozniak, but Jobs deserves credit for the friendly
packaging, the sleekly designed casing, and more importantly, the marketing focus and messaging that brought the
product to consumers with tremendous fanfare. As Regis
McKenna, an early Apple PR consultant, commented, "[T]he
Apple II . . . it would be sitting in hobby shops today were it
not for Jobs."[8]

A wave of entries into the personal computing space followed. Each brought its own unique software and hardware
platform. But in 1981, the industry was transformed as IBM,
in collaboration with key partners (Intel and Microsoft),
introduced the IBM PC. It was an instant success, widely

applauded for its open architecture. The industry rapidly moved toward generating IBM-compatible software and hardware. Cheaper and faster machines with greater storage capacity quickly came to define competitive success. Competing platforms rapidly disappeared, and fifteen years of intense competition between PC and software manufacturers ensued.

But Jobs adhered to a very different set of performance dimensions, reflecting a very different theory of value creation. That theory not only guided Apple's subsequent strategy in computing, but defined a succession of future moves and choices. It took on greater clarity with time, but essentially held that *consumers would pay a premium for ease of use, reliability, and elegant design in computing and later other digital devices, and that the best means for delivering this was a relatively closed system with significant vertical integration and heavy investment in effective design.*

Like Walt Disney's theory, Steve Jobs's theory possessed all three strategic sights. It offered clear *foresight* about the evolution of customer tastes and Apple's capacity to shape those tastes. Jobs recognized that computers would become a consumer good. Unlike competitors, he believed that consumers would appreciate aesthetics and aspired to create a device with the elegance of a Porsche or a well-designed kitchen appliance.

Job's *insight* was that the internal capability most critical to value creation in this competitive terrain was design. Of course, this was partly a reflection of his interests and personality. Jobs thought of himself as an artist—obsessed with color, finish, and shape—but he transferred this obsession to the technology as well. Unlike his competitors, Jobs insisted on full control of a closed system—maintaining a tight rein on Apple's technology and any complementary software or hardware. As his biographer, Walter Issacson, comments: "He got hives, or worse, when even contemplating great Apple software running on another company's crappy hardware, and he likewise was allergic to the thought of unapproved apps or content polluting the perfection of an Apple device."[9] In pursuing this heavy focus on design, Apple made large R&D investments, much larger in percentage terms than those of any of its competitors.

Jobs's theory also provided *cross-sight* in that it helped him identify external assets and resources that Apple could use in building this capacity to design products that were elegant and easy to use. Early on, during a fateful visit to Xerox PARC, Jobs recognized the tremendous value in Xerox's graphical user interface (GUI). The software system that Xerox had developed was astounding, particularly given the current alternative, where navigation occurred through typed commands at the C:> prompt. The key technology engine behind the GUI, as well as the elegant fonts and the remarkable graphics it supported—was *bitmapping* technology, in which the computer controlled individual pixels separately. During his visit, Jobs repeatedly expressed incredulity that Xerox was not commercializing the technology. He recognized that it was a path to introducing computing to the masses through an elegant and easy-to-use device—in other words, he realized that the value of the technology lay in the fact that it could powerfully complement and support good design. The fact that others had failed to see such value reflects the truly contrarian nature of Jobs's theory. The value seems obvious today, of course, but it was much less obvious back in the 1970s, when personal computers were seen by many a toy for nerdy enthusiasts with potential business applications rather than as mass-market electronic consumer goods and major drivers of personal productivity. What then transpired was perhaps one of the greatest technology thefts in history, as the Xerox technology, commercialized first by Apple (and then Microsoft) would revolutionize computing.[10]

The Macintosh was the first fully formed embodiment of Jobs's theory, and it garnered wide acclaim and remarkably high margins (as Jobs predicted). But the IBM standard was already well established, and the PC's network economics were overwhelming. Although the Mac thrived as a profitable niche product, the obvious strategic move for Apple, advocated by Bill Gates and many others, was to port the look and feel of the Macintosh operating system to the IBM platform. But Jobs had no interest in this move, nor any other move to adopt the competing, open-system standard. Any such action was completely inconsistent with his theory.

For more than fifteen years, that decision was derided and second-guessed. The received wisdom was that Apple had made terrible mistakes in not opening its system, not selling windows-based software for the IBM PC, not broadly selling its printers for IBM-compatible PCs, and not selling networking products for the IBM platform. The claim was that Apple could have been Microsoft in software, HP in printers, and Novell or Cisco in networking, and that Apple had squandered its remarkable resources, capabilities, and technical platforms. Jobs was even banished from the company for more than a decade, in part for his dogged insistence on sticking to his theory.

Yet it was Jobs who had the last laugh, and his return to Apple in 1996, shortly after the entire struggling enterprise had been shopped to HP, Sun, and even IBM, is now the stuff of corporate legend. Most observers anticipated that Jobs would simply dress the company up for sale. Instead, he re-imposed his theory with a vengeance, trimming the product range and introducing a new line of Macintosh products not available for license. More important, he used his theory to explore terrain adjacent to personal computing, using the theory's remarkable cross-sight to spot other consumer electronic devices where design and ease of use could transform their value. The result was stunningly successful product introductions across a wide-ranging set of categories.

For the most part, Apple's new products did not represent breakthrough technology. The company was not the first to conceive of or design a digital music library. It did not invent the MP3 player, the smartphone, or the tablet computer. But it was the first to craft and configure these devices with elegant, easy-to-use designs; seamlessly linked complementary products and infrastructure; and sophisticated marketing. Apple has demonstrated that Jobs's theory has broad application beyond computing, with industries and product categories ranging from TV, video systems, home entertainment, portable readers, and information delivery—even automotive systems—as possible targets. Thus, like Walt Disney's, Jobs's legacy is not a string of products but rather a theory of value creation developed in a distinct context that positioned Apple to pursue a succession of strategic experiments and actions that have delivered and are predicted to continue delivering value for Apple shareholders, as well as its delighted consumers.

When Strategy Lacks a Theory—AT&T

Not all corporate theories are created equal, however, and some companies never discover a valuable one. The story of AT&T is a case in point.

In 1984, seven regional Bell operating companies (RBOCs) were spun off from AT&T. In this reorganization, AT&T was also barred from supplying local telephone service, and its assets were slashed from $150 billion to $34 billion. AT&T was left with its long-distance business, its manufacturing arm (Western Electric), and its R&D organization, Bell Labs.[11] With no clear path for growth, AT&T needed a new theory of value creation.

Its first strategic actions after the breakup suggest that its leaders had (at least implicitly) a partial theory whereby they would leverage what they perceived as broad managerial competence to invest the considerable cash flow from its long-distance service into diverse acquisitions and new businesses. The difficulty of articulating the implicit foresight, insight, and cross-sight of this theory, however, reveals its deep flaws. For AT&T, the implicit foresight was that the company could spot trends in industries about which it had relatively little knowledge. The implicit insight was a belief that the company had a general management capability that could allow it to effectively manage and infuse value into a rather disparate array of investments. The implicit cross-sight is almost impossible to identify, as the asset being leveraged had such broad application that a vast array of assets were feasible targets. The cross-sight seemed to reflect a simplistic belief that more diversification would generate more value. Over the next several years, the company made investments consistent with this implicit theory. In 1987, it diversified into data networking, pushing its UNIX operating system.[12] In 1990, it entered the financial services arena with the introduction of its Universal Card. In 1991, it purchased NCR Corporation in response to what it viewed as a growing convergence of telecommunications and computing and in the hope that the acquisition would pave AT&T's way to becoming a truly global company. In 1996, AT&T launched an ISP business, Worldnet, aiming to compete directly with AOL.

But the market was distinctly unimpressed, unconvinced that any of these moves would generate new value for the firm. So in 1995, in response to market pressure, AT&T abandoned its diversification theory, announcing that it would divest two key assets: NCR and Lucent Technologies, a move that essentially carved AT&T into three distinct companies. Meanwhile, the core long-distance business continued to decline, accelerated by the Telecommunications Act of 1996, which allowed the RBOCs to compete with AT&T.[13]

At this point, management appeared to switch to a new theory that reflected a belief in the value of acquiring "the last mile" connection to local customers and providing a bundled package of telephone, broadband internet, and cable services. AT&T declared that its goal would be to "connect with consumers over any distance, in any form, to anybody, in anyplace."[14] This theory was clearly more coherent. Its foresight was predicting exploding internet and cable use. Its insight was recognizing the value in owning the connection to the home. Unfortunately, in the near term at least, the cross-sight was more limited, revealing little beyond the value of purchasing this last mile access to the home, precisely the asset its breakup in 1984 had removed. This theory drove a series of costly cable company acquisitions in 1998–1999, totaling more than $80 billion. Unfortunately, the theory was not unique to AT&T, a critical attribute of an effective theory that will be taken up in chapter 2. Other companies possessed similar theories and also saw value in last-mile access, specifically cable assets. Purchase prices therefore reflected this broadly shared vision. The average price that AT&T paid per subscriber exceeded $4,000, a price that could be justified only through very aggressive revenue growth.

At first, the market applauded these moves, driving AT&T's share price to an all-time high of $59 in July 1999. But by May 2000, the company's stock had dipped to $40, putting AT&T's market cap below one of its baby Bell offspring (SBC) for the first time. In September 2000, the company's share price fell to below $30, due in part to continued declines in long-distance revenues. But it also become increasingly clear that profits streams from digital content flowing through these last mile cables could not in the medium term justify the prices paid. Analysts and investors again began calling for strategic change, in particular an unwinding of the current bundled service strategy. As CFO Chuck Noski commented: " . . . in early 2000, the company, on a sum of the parts basis, was undervalued on almost any measure by a meaningful amount."[15] In response, AT&T again began questioning its corporate theory of value creation, or at least its capacity to sell that theory to Wall Street. CEO C. Michael Armstrong expressed extreme frustration at Wall Street's inability to assess the value of its distinct lines of business.[16]

On October 25, 2000, "Project Grand Slam" was announced, which essentially abandoned the bundled last-mile theory. AT&T announced it would spin off its wireless and cable units into four separate units. Wireless and cable would become separate companies; the business and consumer units would remain under the same roof, but conduct separate operations with the consumer unit's performance linked to a tracking stock (a security that trades on the basis of a subunit's performance). The plan was for these four pieces to share the AT&T brand.

The end of AT&T's quest for a workable theory of value creation came five years later when the organization finally decided that other firms could create more value with its remaining assets than it could itself, and put itself up for sale. It was implicitly a statement that AT&T believed others' theories of what to do with AT&T's assets, when coupled with the assets and capabilities they owned, exceeded any value that AT&T

could create with its own theory. In 2005, AT&T, once the largest company in the world was purchased by SBC, an amalgam of several of the Baby Bells spun off from AT&T, and the entire company was renamed at&t. In a humorous account of the company's many complex changes over the years, comedian Steven Colbert commented that, "Thanks to the country's antitrust efforts, the company has gone from this, AT&T, to this, at&t."

LESSONS LEARNED

The central point of this chapter is a simple one. While sustained value creation demands a relentless search for new complementary bundles of assets and businesses, sustained success in this search demands a well-articulated corporate theory. Absent such a theory, strategic actions are little more than a random walk. The psychologist Kurt Lewin famously commented, "There is nothing as practical as a good theory."[17] Theories provide unique vision; they reveal promising strategic experiments—experiments likely to generate value. Well-crafted theories provide three specific forms of sight:

- **Foresight** into market tastes, opportunities, and technologies.

- **Insight** into which unique assets and resources the firm must own or leverage in order to best exploit its foresight.

- **Cross-sight** into which assets and investment opportunities currently outside the firm are consistent with its foresight and represent good complements to the existing assets and capabilities of the firm.

A theory's sight enables thought experiments: *If my theory accurately describes my world, then when I select this strategic choice, the following will occur.* A theory can be dynamic and can be updated on the basis of contrary evidence or feedback. Just as academic theories enable scientists to generate breakthrough knowledge, corporate theories are the genesis of value-creating strategic actions. They provide the vision necessary to step into uncharted terrain, guiding the selection of what are necessarily uncertain strategic experiments.

As I discuss in chapter 2, vital to a theory's capacity to generate value is the uniqueness of sight it provides. Theories effective in sustaining value creation reveal value in assets uniquely available to the firm. Otherwise, your firm will acquire assets at prices that leave no value on the table to appropriate. Let's look at why this is so.

CHAPTER 2

The Uniqueness
Imperative

T he real power of a well-crafted corporate theory
becomes evident as companies go shopping for the
assets to test their theories. Value creation through
markets always comes down to prices paid, and a good corporate theory enables the acquirer to spot bargains that are
uniquely discerned or uniquely available to it. Mittal Steel is a
good example. From its origin in 1976 until 1989, Mittal Steel
was a very small player in a global steel industry plagued by
low profitability. Its operations consisted solely of a small mill
in Indonesia. Mittal applied a then-new iron ore input technology (direct reduced iron, or DRI) to produce steel and afterward simply expanded with the economic growth of Indonesia.

Then in 1989, Mittal acquired a troubled steel operation
owned by the government of Trinidad and Tobago—a mill
that was operating at 25 percent capacity and losing $1 million

45

per week. Mittal quickly and successfully turned around this business by transferring knowledge from Indonesia, deploying the DRI technology, and expanding sales. What followed was a succession of very significant acquisitions over the next fifteen years, primarily of assets in the former Soviet bloc. Each proved a gold mine.

Guiding this succession of acquisitions was a clear and simple corporate theory. To other steel firms, many of which were focused on improving their internal operations, the acquisition of state-owned steel operations in the former Soviet bloc was almost unthinkable. But Mittal believed it had the skills to create value from poorly understood and poorly managed state-owned steel operations in developing economies where demand for steel was predicted to escalate. Mittal's theory possessed all three sights. Its foresight was an early recognition of the globalization of the steel industry, escalation in global demand, and the value of iron ore deposits. Its insight was recognizing the value of its DRI technology and its capability to turn around formerly state-owned enterprises. Its cross-sight was to recognize that most steel operations in place in emerging markets were *uniquely* complementary to Mittal's capabilities. While other efficient steel mill operators focused on building and operating mini-mills dependent on scrap metal, Mittal's iron ore–based DRI technology, its turnaround skills, and its willingness and competence in operating in emerging markets were unparalleled. To Mittal, these targeted assets were outright bargains.

By 2004, Mittal had emerged as the world's largest and lowest-cost steel producer. Lakshmi Niwas Mittal, its key owner, became one of the world's wealthiest individuals. Mittal's success came from having a corporate theory that functioned as a remarkable treasure map, revealing assets uniquely valuable to it. Unfortunately, in 2006, Mittal pursued and acquired a very large and well run target—Arcelor, then the world's largest steel producer by revenues and the second largest by tons shipped—paying a massive premium in the process. This move was quite inconsistent with its historic theory. The acquisition was also ill-timed: the financial crisis hit, followed by several years of falling steel prices as demand flattened and Chinese capacity came online. While all steel companies have struggled in this new era, Mittal's deviation from its theory of buying troubled assets in emerging markets saddled it with large debt and the costs of integrating a massive asset inconsistent with its historic skills.

The mark of a well-crafted corporate theory is the uniqueness of the value-creating opportunities it reveals. This uniqueness may stem from the uniqueness of the foresight the theory reveals or from the uniqueness of the assets and capabilities a company already possesses. In this chapter, I'll explain the market dynamics that make this uniqueness so necessary to value creation and discuss the pivotal role that a corporate theory plays in revealing this value.

It's All about Auctions

Assets and capabilities are found in a bewildering array of places. Managers shop for skills and knowledge in labor markets. They shop for parts, services, and other inputs in supply markets. They shop for technology in patent and licensing markets. They solicit financial resources in financial markets. More broadly, they search for any critical complementary assets and resources in a range of markets, including the market for entire firms—the acquisitions and mergers market. This activity is staggering in scope, since the range of possible combinations to assemble through markets for people, technology, and assets is nearly infinite. The manager is essentially on a massive treasure hunt where the landscape, the value of hidden treasure, and the map to find it are all unique to a given firm.

The 2010 Nobel Prize in economics was awarded Peter Diamond, Dale Mortenson, and Christopher Pissarides for pioneering work on this type of problem. They argued that many of the markets in which managers participate are "matching markets." For instance, in labor markets, employers place widely divergent value on the skill sets of particular individuals. Individual workers in turn place widely divergent value on working for different employers. An effective matching market optimally pairs employers to workers in a pattern that maximizes the total value generated.

Managers confront an array of highly complex matching markets as they search for value-creating bargains. These bargains reflect matches where buyers procure assets from sellers at market prices and yet still generate value. Exceptional financial returns in all settings are ultimately "rewards for scarcity"; in other words, value creation arising from finding a scarce and valuable match between your firm and available assets—a match that others cannot see or cannot access.[1]

This sounds obvious, but finding such matches is extremely difficult. Almost any business school lecture on M&A (a common way for firms to acquire assets and capabilities) begins with the empirical observation that the average corporate acquisition fails to deliver value for acquiring firms. More precisely, research suggests that on the day of an announced acquisition (or perhaps a few days before or after it), the capital market response is on average slightly negative—a response that suggests the market perceives on average slight overpayment.[2]

To understand why this happens, we need to step back and look at what all the resource markets have in common. Essentially, they are all variants of an auction process. Sellers submit assets for sale, while buyers submit purchase bids, and the auction process then matches the buyers to the sellers. Buyers create value when they obtain assets at a discount relative to their future, deployed use. Two impediments make discovering underpriced assets tremendously difficult. One, created by the uncertainty in calculating value, is known as "winner's curse." The other impediment is that firms can capture value in auctions only from the unique value they create when they acquire the target and not from any common value that other acquirers can also create. Because of the critical importance of these two impediments to value creation in corporate strategy, let's look at the logic of each.

Auctions and the Winner's Curse

Most of us have at one time felt what's called *the winner's curse*, the dismaying realization, upon winning an auction, that no one else thinks the asset just acquired was worth the price you paid.[3] You know this is true because if it were not, higher bids would have been placed.

The winner's curse results from the simple fact that estimates of value in auctions are just that: estimates. As a consequence, those with the most wrong—or specifically those with the most upwardly wrong—estimates "win" auctions. The winners' curse is pervasive in *common value* auctions—where the "true" value of an asset is identical for all bidders, but each bidder estimates this value with considerable error. Suppose five firms are competing for an acquisition target that is completely unrelated to their other assets. In this case, only the stand-alone assessments of value are relevant. But let's assume that though their average estimate of value is accurate, the bids are randomly distributed around this average. In this case, the "successful" bidder—the firm with the highest (over)estimate of value—overpays by the difference between the overestimated value and the true value. Savvy bidders may seek to avoid the winner's curse by shading their bids downward—submitting bids that are below their actual estimate of the value of the item. But unless all bidders are exceptionally disciplined and sufficiently self-aware so as to recognize the scope of their potential overvaluation, then winners overpay and the winner's curse prevails.

What's more, the severity of the winner's curse is likely to increase with the number of bidders. The more bidders there are, the greater the likelihood that some will substantially overestimate the value of the item on auction. Consistent with this logic, empirical evidence suggests that as the number of bidders in an acquisition auction increases, the capital market's response to an announced acquisition becomes more negative.[4]

What about synergies?

But, of course, in purchasing assets, firms seldom participate in common value auctions. Instead, bidders possess private values, which reflect their unique foresight and cross-sight into which assets are uniquely complementary to their core assets (as recognized by insight). Thus, an organization may place particular value on an asset that uniquely complements the firm's own assets. Or, a firm's unique theory may reveal value in a particular configuration of assets that others do not recognize. Under these circumstances, firms are able to provide differing bids, win auctions, and still retain value. By buying and selling assets in competitive markets while guided by unique corporate theories and uniquely complementary assets, they may continually discover value-creating targets at "bargain prices."

However, under these circumstances, the path to value creation is narrower than might be expected. Consider the simple illustration of an auction for PlumCo, a small independent manufacturer of industrial products. The owners have determined it is time to sell. They retain an investment banker, who develops a sophisticated valuation model, which for purposes of illustration we'll deem to be fully accurate in calculating the stand-alone value. Their model concludes that PlumCo's stand-alone value is $14 million.

Of course, the investment banker and the owner are not very interested in this stand-alone value. They focus instead on the private values that various buyers may assign to to PlumCo as a target—values that reflect the respective buyers' synergies. The investment banker markets PlumCo to companies that are particularly well matched—those with strong complementary assets and with the highest private values— and discovers five bidders with significant complementary assets: Alpha Industries, Beta Products, Gamma Systems, Delta Investors, and Epsilon Inc.

Alpha Industries examines PlumCo and recognizes that exceptional value could be gained by distributing its products through Alpha's distribution channels. Alpha conducts its own sophisticated valuation and concludes that the present value of this enhanced performance is worth an additional $2 million, for a total value of $16 million. Beta Products assesses its own internal assets and sees a valuable distribution channel comparable to Alpha, but additionally recognizes valuable technology by which PlumCo's products can be significantly enhanced. Beta performs its valuation and concludes that the combined value of these two synergies is worth an additional $3 million, or $17 million total. Gamma Systems assesses its complementary assets and recognizes that in addition to having assets similar to those possessed by Beta Products, it has marketing skills uniquely suited to PlumCo's product portfolio. Sigma estimates the total value of these synergies at $4 million, for a total value of $18 million. Delta Investors turns out to have all of Sigma's synergies, but also valuable R&D technology that it believes will enhance PlumCo's product portfolio, and its estimates place the total value generated by these synergies at $6 million, for a total value of $20 million. Finally, Epsilon Inc., in addition to commanding the same synergies with PlumCo as Delta Investors, additionally possesses some idle production capacity that will lower PlumCo's production costs. Epsilon estimates that the total value of its synergies is worth $7 million, for a total value of $21 million.

In an ensuing auction, Epsilon Inc. presumably obtains the target for a price above $20 million, but below $21 million. At any price below $20 million, Delta Investors will be willing to bid more, but at prices above $20 million, Delta drops out. What portion of the $7 million in synergies between Epsilon and PlumCo does Epsilon capture? At best, it retains somewhere between zero and $1 million. All of the remaining $6 million-plus in synergies—the value of all synergies that are non-unique—accrue to PlumCo's shareholders.

The moral of the tale is that even in these "private value" auctions, where bidders' valuations of the target reflect their unique theories and assets, the winning bidder captures at most the privately held unique value it possesses with the target (as illustrated in figure 2-1).

Of course, the example above is extremely simplified. In a real auction, the synergies that bidders possess with the target

FIGURE 2-1

Asset auctions with synergies

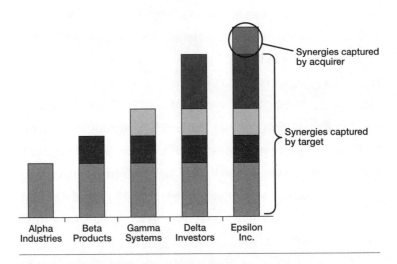

Alpha Industries | Beta Products | Gamma Systems | Delta Investors | Epsilon Inc.

Synergies captured by acquirer

Synergies captured by target

are not as nicely additive. Rather, each would-be acquirer has a unique composition of synergies. Some will have better distribution assets, others better technology, and others more valuable brands. However, the fundamental principle remains: the maximum value retained by the winning bidder is the difference between the value of that bidder's synergies with the target and the synergy valuation of the bidder with the next-highest valuation. Again, the maximum appropriation by the buyer is the portion of synergies that are unique. The value of the remaining shared synergies flows to the target shareholders.

What happens if each bidder also estimates the value of synergies with considerable error? Many firms are prone to substantially overbid for the real synergies that they possess, especially because confidence—the belief that they can pull off a difficult challenge or that they know their business better than others—is a key attribute of effective leaders. But confident leaders are prone to exaggerate the value they can generate with targets. Clearly, in these circumstances, discovering value-creating acquisitions is highly problematic.

So what was it that set Mittal's apart? How did it, for so long, consistently avoid overpaying for new assets? The answer is simple. Mittal developed a corporate theory that revealed target assets with which it uniquely possessed synergies. Other companies did not have those synergies. Consequently, Mittal could participate in the auction markets, win assets in these auctions, and still appropriate tremendous value.

The Importance of Being Unique

Of course, many theories prove to be misguided and value-destroying. They reveal flawed foresight, skewed insight about existing assets, or cross-sight that overestimates synergies. In most cases, however, these faults stem from a single cause: *the theory has not identified anything unique.*

Consider the saga of General Mills as it aggressively pursued an array of acquisitions in the 1970s and 1980s. In the early 1970s, General Mills discarded its flour-milling assets and developed a new theory of value creation prompted in part by a senior faculty retreat entitled "Good to Great." The result was a plan to diversify through acquisition into new businesses, businesses not only beyond packaged foods, but businesses with a bit more flair and excitement than Bisquick and Cheerios. The companies it acquired fell largely into five broad categories: toys, fashion, restaurants, catalog retailing, and packaged foods.

In making these acquisitions, General Mills appeared to have a reasonably clear theory of its path to value creation—one they believed would enable the purchase of assets at prices below their future value as deployed within General Mills. The implicit theory was that General Mills had a deep understanding of household consumers, including what direction their tastes and preferences were taking, and a broadly applicable skill in consumer goods marketing, which it could use to infuse value into a wide range of consumer goods businesses. Perhaps equally important, there was an idea that combining or collecting related assets under these five platforms was value-creating.

At first glance, this theory was not lacking in merit. General Mills was a reasonably good marketer, and the assets it had purchased indicated that it had a good sense of trending consumer tastes and preferences. In terms of cross-sight, it was possible to see some modest potential synergies between consumer goods and restaurants, or even between toys and packaged foods.

The trouble is, none of these sights was unique. They revealed neither internal uniqueness that General Mills could leverage nor unique value-creating opportunities it could pursue. General Mills did not have any skills or assets that competing acquirers did not, and other firms shared its views on where consumer tastes were heading. While some of their investments in toys (e.g., Kenner's Star Wars products) or fashion (Izod and the emerging preppy look in the late 1970's) proved clairvoyant, General Mills seemed as surprised by these successes as anyone.

Nor did General Mills have any unique complementarity to the assets it acquired. Other bidders for the acquired assets likely possessed equal if not greater knowledge, capabilities, or even physical assets with greater synergies with these targets. Toy firms, specialty catalog retailers, or even restaurant chains were arguably better positioned to give ongoing strategic guidance to fashion companies than executives in the food product industry.

Consequently, aggregate purchase prices paid by General Mills very likely exceeded the anticipated value of cash flows, which probably explains General Mills' unimpressive stock price performance between 1974 and 1984, a period in which it significantly underperformed the S&P 500. The clear lesson is that buying assets at prices below their deployed value requires having a theory that reveals more than generic synergies. It requires a unique theory.

But to fully understand the challenges faced in creating value through acquisitions and the central role of uniqueness, we need to look at the process from the seller's perspective.

The Virtues of Selling and the Challenges of Buying

When corporate theories are common—when they reveal only commonly held foresight and identify synergies easily accessed by other firms, then selling assets has clear advantages, while buying has a much more limited upside. Consider the events that played out in the US defense industry as the Cold War came to a close. In 1989, the Soviet-backed regimes in Hungary, East Germany, Bulgaria, Romania, and Czechoslovakia all fell. In November 1990, presidents George H. W. Bush and Mikhail Gorbachev announced the official end of the Cold War. Almost instantly, expectations regarding defense spending collapsed—the 1991 and 1992 US defense budgets declined 25 percent from 1990 levels. The market value for all defense contractors also collapsed as they confronted a very different strategic landscape—one in which organic sales growth afforded little opportunity for value creation. Suddenly, consolidation became the clear path to value creation (or at least the path to reducing further value erosion). However, this same theory was rather clear to every defense contractor and the key question was whether your theory was to buy or sell.

The value-creating benefits of selling were compelling. As noted above, in common value auctions, buyers have great difficulty creating any value and may substantially overbid, thereby generating a winners' curse. In private value auctions, buyers retain only the unique value they can derive from the assets they purchase—that is, they capture at most the value of any unique synergies, while the value of the remaining or common synergies flows to the seller. Although there were certainly firms in the defense industry with differing assets and thus potentially unique synergies, there was also much commonality and overlap. Indeed, over the years, to encourage competition, the government explicitly supported multiple firms in areas such as missiles, aircraft, space systems, and defense electronics. Consequently, there were multiple bidders with potentially significant synergies with any given asset or acquisition on offer.

In 1989, William Anders became chairman and CEO of General Dynamics, which at the time was the second-largest US defense contractor. His contract included an incentive package that strongly rewarded share price appreciation. Along with others in the industry, he quickly saw the need for consolidation, but he was rather alone among the larger defense contractors in recognizing (or at least recognizing and acting upon) the fact that selling afforded much greater returns than buying. From late 1991 to late 1993, General Dynamics sold its data systems, small commercial aircraft (Cessna), missiles, electronics, military aircraft, and space systems divisions. For the most part, all of these sales were made to strategic buyers in the defense industry with similar assets, or in the case of data systems, to a large IT consulting firm. Consequently, General Dynamics was positioned as a seller to nearly fully capture the synergies buyers possessed, as these substantial synergies available to buyers were rather non-unique.

As a result of these strategic sales and other cost-cutting moves, between 1991 and 1993 General Dynamics shareholders received a 553 percent return, or $4.5 billion in additional value on a base of about $1 billion in 1991. Quite a remarkable return—and one largely based on simply capturing the non-unique synergies that bidders had with the General Dynamics assets.

I am not advocating that simply selling assets is the optimal path to sustained value creation for most corporations. After all, at some point a company will run out of assets to sell. And success with such a path was in some ways unique to the opportunity landscape that confronted defense contractors in 1991. However, this illustration does provide a cautionary tale about the challenges that firms face in asset procurement. As noted, firms pursuing acquisitions will distribute all non-unique synergies to acquirers. Therefore, it is essential that acquirers have a unique and ultimately accurate theory that enables them to identify underpriced assets—assets with which they possess unique complements. Without these, a firm has no path to value creation other than selling assets to others and essentially capturing the non-unique complementarity that others can gain from the assets it possesses. However, as the General Dynamics example shows, this path can be an enormously value-creating one. Managers should not wed themselves to growth as the sole path to value creation.

Lessons from Empirics

How difficult it is to find bargains while assembling assets and resources is easily highlighted by empirical work on acquisition outcomes. One metric for assessing whether a firm has discovered a "bargain" is to examine how capital markets respond to the announcement of an acquisition, which typically includes the purchase price. We can think of this market reaction as a crowdsourced assessment of the price paid relative to the value that investors anticipate will be created. A drop in share price signals that the market perceives over-payment, while a positive response essentially signals a bar-gain. Here is what we know from research of this type:[5]

- **Averaged out, market reactions are not dramatic.**
  Overall, the market's reaction to announced acqui-sitions is slightly negative, suggesting that acquiring firms only slightly overpay for the value obtained. While this suggests the acquisition game is difficult, the result is not surprising. If the average market response were widely positive, this would only encour-age more acquisitions, perhaps more marginal or questionable acquisitions that would lower returns. Similarly, a significantly negative response on average would strongly discourage acquisitions, and as acquisi-tion behavior changed, returns would elevate.

- **The variation is wide.** Although the average market reaction is slightly negative, firms don't pursue the "average acquisition." Many acquisitions trigger a strongly positive market reaction, while others create a strongly negative one. While the average is slightly negative, the variance is tremendous. A recent study suggests that nearly 45 percent of firms saw their stock prices move more than 10 percent positively or negatively in response to an announced acquisition.[6] The result merely highlights the critical role of a corporate theory in ensuring value creation through acquisitions.

- **The lower the premium paid, the more positive the reaction.** In the case of acquisitions of publicly traded firms, when the market's reaction is positive, the average price premium paid was 30.7 percent. When the market's reaction is negative, the average price premium paid was 38.4 percent.[7] Higher premiums are likely to occur in common value auctions where bidders possess synergies with the target that many others bidders also possess. Lower premiums are likely to result from private value auctions where unique corporate theories reveal private value to the acquiring firm.

- **Private information helps**. Research also suggests that the market reacts more positively to the announcement of acquisitions when the targets are privately held firms (or divisions of public firms) rather than publicly traded firms.[8] Because less information is available about privately held firms, there is more opportunity for foresighted and insightful corporate theories to identify valuable acquisitions that others cannot see or access. Scarce information means those with equally complementary assets are less likely to also spot them and bid away the opportunity for value creation.

- **Firms pursuing more "unique" corporate strategies pay less for their acquisition targets.** My own research with Lubomir Litov shows that having a unique corporate theory (and presumably the unique foresight or cross-sight that such a theory provides) enables firms to pay discounted prices for the assets that they purchase.[9] We find that as firms move from the tenth to the ninetieth percentile in terms of our strategic uniqueness measure, the price declines from an average premium of 34 percent to an average premium of 20 percent. As discussed above, lower premiums increase the probability that the market will perceive an acquisition as value creating.

Investing with a Theory

Acquisitions are, of course, only one of the vehicles through which firms pursue theory-guided strategic investments. More broadly, firms pursue investments such as hiring talent, building factories, investing in R&D, and acquiring licenses to technology. Making effective choices from among a vast array of investment options is vital to sustaining value creation.

In most firms, the process of comparatively evaluating investments can feel very much like a beauty contest. The details may vary, but the basic process is this: Contestants from disparate groups and subunits of the firm put together investment ideas, forecast their value, and draft compelling proposals to lure the attention of those judging them. Proposals are then filtered and distilled down to a set that is passed up to the corporate level for review. What follows are often culminating events in which these groups or individuals parade in front of senior managers or the board to make their pitch. Senior management must then comparatively assess the merits of what amount to strategic experiments with often very uncertain outcomes.

To guide that assessment, decision makers are generally advised to apply a rather straightforward rule for evaluating investments of any type: say yes to projects that have a positive net present value (NPV). The math to calculate NPV is likely familiar: estimate a project's future cash flows net of investment (both positive and negative), "discount" these cash flows to the present, using the current cost of accessing capital, and sum them. If the calculation is positive, invest. If not, pass. Given such a straightforward decision rule, why bother with a corporate theory?

Part of the answer is that although the math to calculate NPV is simple, generating the inputs for calculation—the forecasts of future returns is not. In fact, all such forecasts are necessarily business fiction, and there are no limits on imagination or on the cognitive and behavioral distortions that may fuel it. One large company I advised discovered from a post mortem analysis that its aggregate return on newly invested capital from 2008 to 2013, all of which were positive NPV, was significantly negative. Its investments had destroyed rather than created value.

This is not unusual. All too often, projections of future returns are upwardly biased. Partly this reflects proposers' optimism about their capacity to create value from the investments they propose. While such confidence is perhaps an attribute essential to putting together a strong proposal in the first place, proposers may also have incentives to deliberately inflate projections: the battle for resources has personal implications—the success of a proposal shapes personal credibility, remuneration, and career prospects. In fact, competing proposals often lead to an arms race of exaggerated claims and projections. The only tempering effect is the hit that failure to deliver has on proposers' future capacity to obtain funds. Therefore, given the necessarily fictional nature of proposals, those evaluating them must make a subjective decision about whose fiction they prefer—whose narrative of the future they find most compelling.

This is where a good corporate theory becomes particularly vital as a tool for selecting the right alternative hypotheses or fictions. As with acquisitions, theory-guided investment may enable the purchase, formation, and structuring of valuable activities and assets at discounted prices—for instance, hiring talent, designing activities and routines, and contracting for others—before rising demand for these investments escalates prices, as your foresighted corporate theory predicts it should. Theory-guided investment may also grant a firm a temporary advantage—for instance, a technological position that is difficult for others to quickly replicate, and leaves them to play a costly game of catch-up.

Monsanto's investment history is illustrative. In 1983 Richard Mahoney took over as CEO of what is now the agricultural biotechnology giant. At the time Mahoney became CEO, Monsanto was a chemical company and, under his predecessor, had only dabbled in biotechnology. Mahoney had a theory that biotech was the future in both pharmaceuticals and agriculture, and he decided to transition into these sectors. The approach was to generate cash by selling most of the petrochemicals businesses and squeezing additional cash from other businesses, thereby enabling heavy investment in biotechnology and industries that could utilize it. Mahoney's vision was a "life sciences" company that could explore the health and healing of humans, the genetic functioning of plants, and the composition of food. The theory projected foresight about the value of biotechnology, insight into the value (or lack thereof) of existing assets and capabilities, and articulated clear cross-sight concerning investments in talent, technology, and assets to access or acquire.

In his first year as CEO, Mahoney sold off Monsanto's commodity chemical, paper, and polystyrene divisions, which accounted for about $4 billion in sales. Between 1985 and 1990, he sold off an additional eighteen business units and made several acquisitions, most notably a pharmaceutical firm, the Searle Corporation, which included Nutrasweet. Monsanto then invested heavily in specialty chemicals, agricultural products, pharmaceuticals, and biotechnology. Central to investment in these latter three businesses was the formation of a central lab focused on biotechnology and the hiring of an army of post-docs charged with doing research in areas such as the genetic structure of plants, the molecular science of taste, and the functioning of the stomach. While the broad vision of a life sciences company was composed centrally, the specific projects and investment paths were locally proposed and reviewed for their consistency with this theory.

In other words, it wasn't that Monsanto avoided the need for a beauty contest, it was merely that the set of acceptable proposals was filtered by the theory. Accordingly, Monsanto began heavily investing in both pharma with the purchase of Searle and agricultural biotech R&D. By the mid-1980s, Monsanto had developed several important breakthroughs critical to modifying the genetic structure of plants. These tools were then used to develop products of enormous value to farmers, such as seeds that produced plants resistant to the herbicide glyphosate (or Roundup) or plants that were resistant to destructive insects. Both technologies dramatically reshaped the economics of farming and reduced the need for environmentally unfriendly herbicides and insecticides.

Although this unique theory of heavily investing in biotech, particularly agricultural biotech, was controversial at the time and actively resisted by many analysts (and environmentalists), Mahoney's investment decisions were remarkably foresighted. Monsanto's investments in pharmaceuticals and the purchase of Searle paid off quickly. In 1993, Searle filed patents for the first selective COX-2 inhibitor that became the blockbuster drug Celebrex (the drug that prompted Pharmacia to purchase Monsanto in 1999). Recognition of the agricultural biotech investments took longer. Despite the development of both Roundup-ready corn and soy, Mahoney's large investment in agricultural biotechnology was initially seen as a waste of money. But fifteen years later, these initial large investments in ag biotech and those that followed had generated enormous value for investors. Of course, competitors like DuPont and Ciba-Geigy eventually recognized ag biotech's potential, but by that point

Monsanto's technological lead was formidable. Competitors were left to play a very costly game of catch-up, and none have competed particularly well.

One of the real advantages of a corporate theory is its capacity to help senior managers overcome their own inherent biases in evaluating investments. Senior managers are all too often inclined toward divvying resources up more evenly than is optimal or simply carrying last year's investment pattern forward. Alternatively, they may go entirely hands off and allow business units to retain and invest whatever excess cash they generate. Or, they may adopt a simplifying, but rather ill-conceived portfolio model that preclassifies businesses into investment categories that shapes the types of investments that will be considered by each. All of these are a poor substitute for the critical task of composing a corporate theory and then evaluating the merits of the strategic experiments that it reveals.

Well-crafted theories help managers identify unique, underpriced opportunities for creating value through investment, pinpointing which combination of new and existing assets will create value not yet built into the share price. As illustrated by the case of Monsanto and many other companies, managers must be prepared to stick with their theories until performance proves or disproves the accuracy of their theories and their ability to implement them. Following a theory can also reduce, though it may not eliminate, many of the cognitive and behavioral distortions that plague conventional investment processes. Finally, patterns of investment are a key vehicle through which theories are tested, and through which investors evaluate these theories for their own portfolios.

LESSONS LEARNED

Whether you are acquiring whole corporations or specific assets—or even hiring people—in order to create value, you need to acquire these assets at prices that are less than the value you can create with them. A well-thought-out corporate theory makes spotting such bargains more likely.

The capacity to spot bargains comes from one of two sources. Either cross-sight and foresight reveal complementarity among assets that others cannot see, or insight reveals complements to available assets that you uniquely possess. Either path is entirely about uniqueness. Without this uniqueness in your corporate theory, other firms may well be better at implementing your theory than you are.

However, it is not enough to craft a well-sighted theory that reveals unique complementarities. As the difficulties experienced by Steve Jobs illustrate, the financial markets may not be convinced by a firm's theory, which means that it may never get the chance to test its theory. As we will see in chapter 3, this problem arises precisely because the value in your theory's three unique sights are not obvious or easy to verify, and financial markets are almost structurally conditioned to discount them. Overcoming this problem to successfully sell the theory to investors is the next challenge facing the corporate theory builder.

CHAPTER 3

Moral Hazard or Market for Lemons?

S trategic managers must not only compose valuable corporate theories; they must also finance them.[1] The challenge in finding funds is that investors may have their own beliefs and theories about the optimal path to value creation with the assets and activities an organization controls. They may even question the firm's judgment and motives. Conflicting ideas about the path to value creation and investors' suspicion of managerial motives create a tension that pervades corporate boardrooms and executive suites, not to mention the halls of academe, and presents a real challenge to a company's efforts to compose and pursue a valuable corporate theory.

A fundamental question underlies this tension: Who should ideally set strategic direction—expert managers with deep knowledge of their industries and resources, or an independent "crowd" of investors and their advisers? The answer is not obvious. On the one hand, managers as experts have access to information often unavailable to the market, including extensive knowledge of the resources available and opportunities present in their own organizations. On the other hand, the capital markets aggregate a vast array of disparate opinions of investors (and potential investors) about a firm's proposed actions. Moreover, if an organization's task is to maximize enterprise value, there is clear wisdom in taking strategic actions consistent with investors' beliefs and theories. After all, investors establish the value of the enterprise. Why not give them what they want?

Essentially, the issue that underlies these divergent paths is a problem of agency. Managers are hired to act in investors' interests because they possess information and skills that investors lack—information vital to composing a valuable corporate theory. But managers also have personal interests in selecting the corporate theory that may diverge from the simple value-maximizing motives of investors. So the choice for owner-investors is either to allow managers—with their self-serving incentives, but presumably better information—to choose the theory, or to maximize their own control by shaping managers' incentives to simply attend to investor signals and feedback, in some sense crowdsourcing the selection of strategic action from the beliefs of investors.

To see what's at stake, let's consider Kraft's unsolicited offer for Cadbury in September 2009. The offer met substantial resistance from Cadbury's board. The UK public voiced its own tremendous resistance—the idea that a US firm would buy this iconic British brand seemed unthinkable. In the face of this resistance, Kraft quickly launched a hostile takeover effort, claiming a host of synergies with Cadbury. The investment community, however, was not convinced that the deal would create value, especially when Warren Buffet, a large shareholder in Kraft, opposed the deal. Kraft's share price dropped in response. Nonetheless, in January 2010, the Cadbury board agreed to terms with Kraft and the deal was consummated. This agreement only amplified the market's negative response. Though Kraft's stock rose 5 percent from the time of its initial proposal to the final agreement, Kraft's shares generally responded negatively, given that the S&P 500 rose 15 percent over this same period.[2]

The acquisition did little to dissuade the more active of Kraft's investors from pushing for a strategy revision. The hedge fund Pershing Square Capital accumulated significant shares and began pressuring Kraft to rethink its bundle of businesses. Then, just eighteen months after its acquisition of Cadbury, Kraft announced that it was splitting its more stable, slower-growth grocery products like Oscar Meyer, Jell-O, Maxwell House, and Kraft Macaroni & Cheese into a separate business from the faster-growing snack brands. In doing so, Kraft pushed to "unlock value."[3] The capital market's response was predictably positive.

Who was in charge of Kraft's strategy? Was it managers using their superior knowledge to create a corporate theory and execute strategy? Or were investors in charge, pushing managers to forgo what investors perceived as empire-building, value-destroying moves? The question reveals the existence of two very different philosophies about the motivation and roles of managers in the value-creation process. Understanding their difference is vital to understanding your role as a manager in sustaining value creation.

Moral Hazard: Managers as Villains

The philosophy that pervades Wall Street and dominates the academic finance literature emphasizes the remarkable and well-documented efficiency of prices in capital markets as a guide to strategic choice. Friedrich Hayek long ago argued that the "marvel of the market" is its capacity to assemble the collective wisdom of dispersed actors in markets and to essentially send powerful signals to managers about the merits of their strategic choices.[4]

This genius is well illustrated by capital markets' rapid and accurate response following the *Challenger* disaster. While NASA launched an extensive five-month investigation pinpointing the proximate cause as supplier Morton-Thiokol's defective O-rings, the capital markets fingered Thiokol on the very day of the disaster. Within twenty-four hours, Thiokol's share price plummeted 12 percent, while the other large contractors on the project saw much more modest reductions in value. Capital markets may be equally skilled in evaluating strategic choices, or even the merits of a corporate theory.

So why not defer to the wisdom of capital markets in selecting strategy?[5]

From the capital markets perspective, the manager's task is reduced to deciphering market signals and responding strategically. This position would argue that Kraft's managers destroyed value when they ignored the market's negative signals and pushed forward with the purchase of Cadbury. They generated value when they responded to investors' signals and separated out the slow-growing grocery business from the remaining assets. Thus, managers create value when they pursue strategies consistent with the wisdom of the crowd and destroy value when they ignore it.

The core challenge in this worldview is ensuring that managers follow market signals. Investors therefore seek to shape managers' incentives so that they attend to investors' interests and beliefs about the path to value rather than their personal interests or beliefs. This approach was most explicitly articulated by Michael Jensen and William Meckling, who in a pathbreaking 1976 article delineated the fundamental agency problem, often called *moral hazard*, in which managers pursue personal interests rather than the interests of principals.[6]

Many experts credited the rapid growth of large conglomerates in the 1960s to this phenomenon. With their salaries strongly linked to the size of the enterprise they managed, managers favored weak corporate theories that privileged organizational size over value creation. A lack of incentives to focus on shareholder value caused managers to craft flawed theories aimed at building empires that yielded private benefits but compromised value.

To sum up, in the capital markets perspective, investors are assumed to be highly efficient in their capacity to gather information, evaluate strategies, and allocate resources. Managers, by contrast, are seen as lazy and/or self-interested. Firm value is therefore increased when managers' pursuit of personal agendas is corrected by imposing equity-based compensation systems that tie managers' incentives to the beliefs and interests of shareholders. Motivated by such incentives, managers choose actions consistent with investors' collective beliefs about value creation.

Managers' self-interested actions may also be corrected by increasing the flow of information to investors about a firm's corporate theory and by creating organizations that use simple, pure plays, operating within a single business—where capital markets can send direct signals to management about the value of actions free from the tangle of multiple strategies and businesses. Empirical evidence suggests that capital markets respond favorably as firms unbundle their strategic combinations and become focused pure plays. From this perspective, the market's favorable response to Kraft's decision to unbundle reflects a belief that the increased incentives and market discipline will somehow elevate performance. Better incentives will in essence "unlock" value previously lost.

The Lemons Problem: When Markets Fail

Powerful as the capital markets perspective is, it is arguably not the primary path to sustained value creation. Instead,

I would argue that the primary path to value creation results from the creative, theory-building capacities of managers—those hired to see things investors often cannot. This strategic perspective (as opposed to the capital markets perspective) also recognizes that the separation of ownership from managerial control creates an agency problem, but unlike the moral hazard problem, here the problem is that well-intentioned and well-informed managers are constantly searching to build value but are frustrated by their inability to convince investors of their superior knowledge and vision. The strategic perspective sees the primary governance challenge as one of curing capital markets of their inability to correctly value firms, rather than curing firms of their lazy or empire-building managers.

Consider again the Kraft example. From the strategic perspective, the CEO's job is to craft a far-seeing, insightful theory that forecasts the evolution of the industry and specifies the complementarity between the assets owned or available for purchase. Here, the CEO's task is to make strategic choices that will maximize the firm's long-run profitability, even if capital markets fail to see this value in the short run. After all, the CEO is hired to be smarter than investors. The challenge is convincing investors this is true—a task made all the more challenging because frequently it simply isn't; sometimes managers' theories are bad, aimed at building empires and not value.

In 2001, George Akerlof received the Nobel Prize in economics for groundbreaking work illuminating our understanding of a more general form of this precise problem.[7]

Akerlof labeled it the "lemons" problem, comparing it to the used-car market, where it is difficult for buyers to know whether the car they are purchasing is of high or low quality.[8] The essence of the general problem is this: in markets where the quality of goods and services cannot be readily observed or measured, sellers, who uniquely know their quality, have incentives to exploit this information advantage to their benefit. They do this by selling indiscernibly low-quality goods in markets that expect and are correspondingly priced for higher-quality goods. While a growing flood of low-quality goods eventually drags down the market price, the interim benefits from offering them may be substantial. Because those who wish to sell high-quality goods have no means to credibly signal their high quality, high quality is simply withheld from the market. As a consequence, the market evolves to the point where it consists only of low-quality "lemons," and all goods sold are heavily discounted.

Managers face an analogous problem in attempting to sell their theories to investors in capital markets. The quality of a corporate theory is massively difficult to assess—the product is a mere cognitive vision of a path to sustained value creation. A more difficult-to-evaluate product is hard to imagine; the true value is unknown even to the manager and is revealed only as "experiments" or strategic actions are pursued over a period of years. Accordingly, managers can all too easily disguise poor-quality theories as high-quality ones.

To overcome this information problem, managers often devote substantial time and resources to convince capital markets of the inherent value of their theories. CEOs of public firms often spend as much as 25 to 30 percent of their time meeting with investors and analysts, in an effort to minimize the information gulf between senior managers and investors. These efforts do not create real value themselves, but instead seek to alter investor perceptions of value, or investor patience as discussed below.

The dot-com boom (and bust) of the late 1990s highlights the potentially troubling consequences of this information gulf. From 1995 to 2000, scores of internet firms emerged with different business models for value creation and capture. Entrepreneur after entrepreneur developed online businesses, articulated strategic messages connecting their models to future value creation, sent out IPO prospectuses, and then solicited investors through public equity offerings. Many of these companies had no revenues. Few, if any, had profits. Nearly all had very vague theories about their path to cash-flow growth. Historical accounting numbers provided no real basis for evaluating the quality of these theoretical businesses. Value in the market was therefore merely a reflection of the subjective assessments of completely untested theories.

What emerged quite predictably was a classic market for lemons. Because the real value of these business models was impossible to assess, market valuations were based on observable "performance" measures. For instance, a 2000 study of dot-com valuations concluded that market valuations were negatively related to net income, but strongly and positively related to hits to the company website and to simple measures of R&D and marketing dollars spent.[9] Far too little attention was focused on the likely future revenue or profit that a hit to the website might garner.

Unsurprisingly, the strategic actions developed by dot-com management teams focused on generating web traffic, to the detriment of strategic thought focused on real value creation. Equally unsurprisingly, the majority of these dot-com theories were revealed to be lemons, grossly deficient in strategic logic and pandering to the web-hit metric that so powerfully shaped valuation. As this reality set in, the market crashed. The difficulty of separating those firms with truly valuable strategies from the lemons became apparent, and even those with compelling strategies and positions, such as Amazon, were sharply discounted.

The lemons problem is not limited to the dot-com model. Managers crafting corporate theories of growth face a very similar information problem as they attempt to sell these theories to investors. These managers are paid to know more than capital markets about the quality and future value of their theories, but they are often incapable of persuasively articulating that inherent future value. As a consequence, high-quality theories paradoxically may be discounted in capital markets, especially when they are difficult to evaluate.

The big problem with such discounting is that managers rely on capital markets for resources to pursue their corporate theories. Perceptions of low quality elevate financing costs. Moreover, managers' compensation and continued employment typically depend on their capacity to generate market value in the present. Thus, this lemons problem leads to a strategic dilemma of massive significance. Managers may be tempted to pander to the beliefs and preferences of the capital markets rather than pursue the corporate theories that would maximize value for the firm.

The Strategy Paradox

Many managers are certainly aware of this dilemma. Over the years, I heard many complaints from CEOs of publicly traded firms such as Boeing, AT&T, Cardinal Health, Aetna, and Tyco that their strategies were being incorrectly valued. Their frustration was often directed at young securities analysts who were either unable or unwilling to dig in and evaluate their complex or unique strategies.

And for many years, I remained firmly convinced of the capital markets perspective and the reliability of collective wisdom in assessing value. I generally dismissed such complaints as scapegoating; placing the blame on analysts seemed to me an excuse for empire building and poor strategic choices. But a question lurked beneath the surface: Was it possible that the CEOs' view was accurate—that capital markets and the market actors that supported them simply had an aversion to the unique, complex, and unfamiliar? The answer to this question is critical, as it fundamentally shapes the path to value creation. Does value creation primarily mandate solving a moral hazard problem by motivating otherwise lazy, greedy, or overconfident CEOs to act in shareholder interests? Or does value creation mandate solving the lemons problem that prevents CEOs with valuable corporate theories from being able to pursue them?

My thinking on this critical dilemma shifted when in 1999 a student sent me an analyst report about his employer, the Monsanto Corporation. At the time, Monsanto was heavily invested in a portfolio of businesses and assets that leveraged biotechnology and chemical sciences to generate innovative food, agriculture, and pharmaceutical products—as noted in chapter 2, a bundle of businesses that it described as "life sciences."

The theory was that these businesses could share common R&D investments and benefit from commonly applicable technology. Also fundamental to this theory was a belief that pharma and agricultural biotechnology were better investment prospects than chemicals. However, by 1999, the capital markets had soured on the theory. Public opposition to agricultural biotechnology, particularly overseas, made ag-biotech a dirty word among investors.

At the same time, Monsanto's pharmaceutical unit generated the anti-arthritis drug Celebrex, which was widely regarded as destined for blockbuster sales. Securities analysts began to press Monsanto management to abandon the strategy of bundling these businesses and investing so heavily in ag-biotech, which they viewed as causing a "valuation drag" on Monsanto's stock. In fact, analysts valued ag-biotech investments, related R&D, and potential future products as practically worthless.

But the report my student sent to me, drafted by Paine Webber, caused me to rethink the logic of the market:

The life sciences experiment is not working with respect to our analysis or in reality. Proper analysis of Monsanto requires expertise in three industries: pharmaceuticals, agricultural chemicals and agricultural biotechnology. Unfortunately, on Wall Street, particularly on the sell-side, these separate industries are analyzed individually because of the complexity of each. This is also true to a very large extent on the buy-side. At PaineWebber, collaboration among analysts brings together expertise in each area. We can attest to the challenges of making this effort pay off: just coordinating a simple thing like work schedules requires lots of effort. While we are willing to pay the price that will make the process work, it is a process not likely to be adopted by Wall Street on a widespread basis. Therefore, Monsanto will probably have to change its structure to be more properly analyzed and valued.[10]

Talk about the tail wagging the dog. This analyst was suggesting that Monsanto incur tens of millions of dollars in investment banking and other transactions fees—not to mention the loss of any synergies—to unbundle the corporation not on the basis of in-depth evaluation or toward real value creation, but because analysts with differing expertise could not coordinate work schedules. Moreover, the report strongly suggested that coverage choices by analysts are based in part on the effort required to provide that coverage. Most importantly, the report directly recommended that the firm dismantle its current strategy to reduce these burdensome information costs for analysts, thereby permitting more extensive and precise analysis, and ultimately raising the overall valuation of the assets.

Interestingly, elsewhere in the report, the analyst applauded Monsanto's history of staying the course despite "heavy resistance from the Street" to change. This was in reference to CEO Dick Mahoney's unwillingness to sell its pharma unit, Searle, in the 1990s when its pipeline looked empty. Of course, events proved that Mahoney possessed foresight in staying the course and that ignoring the analysts then was a good move.

Now in 1999, Monsanto was again at a crossroads. In this instance, however, the CEO played to Wall Street—divisions such as Nutrasweet were sold or spun off, then the remaining entity was sold to Pharmacia, which was in turn quickly acquired by Pfizer. After holding onto the ag-biotech business for the legally required two years, Pfizer spun it off as Monsanto in 2002. Even then, the business was viewed as having rather limited value. Yet the unit's phenomenal subsequent performance has completely exploded this negative judgment. What was nearly valueless to analysts in 1999 turned out to be worth $55 billion in 2013.

This story is only one such anecdote; my experience suggests that managers generally do face a real dilemma as they craft and then sell their corporate theories to capital markets. They can choose simple, familiar strategies that are easy for capital markets to decipher or they can choose complex, unfamiliar, or unique ones based on theories that are difficult to evaluate. In the latter case, valuation is costly, prone to error, and likely leads to a discount in the market.

Figure 3-1 depicts four types of corporate theories that differ along two dimensions: quality and ease of evaluation. Type I theories—theories that are of high quality and easily evaluated—are clearly the preferred choice. However, such theories are unlikely to exist in great abundance since, as discussed, good theories are unique—and unique seldom means easy to evaluate. Type IV theories—theories that are of low quality and relatively opaque—are clearly to be avoided. The majority of options, however, are likely to be type II—theories that are lower in quality and therefore long-term value, but are easily evaluated and therefore may maximize investors' current value—or type III—theories of high quality that maximize long-term value but are difficult to evaluate and are therefore discounted in the present.

FIGURE 3-1

Four types of theories

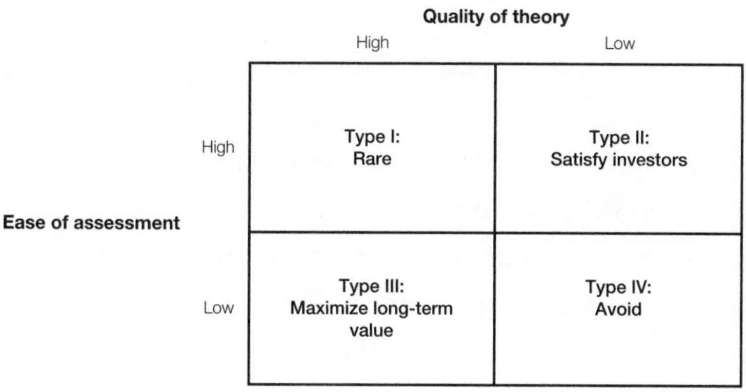

		Quality of theory	
		High	Low
Ease of assessment	High	Type I: Rare	Type II: Satisfy investors
	Low	Type III: Maximize long-term value	Type IV: Avoid

The correct choice is by no means obvious. It is precisely in this quandary that Monsanto found itself.

Securities Analysts and the Costly-to-Analyze Discount

There are actors in capital markets for publicly traded firms who seek to bridge this information gulf and resolve the dilemma. In used-car markets, mechanics and auto dealers certify quality and even function as brokers. In capital markets, there are securities analysts who specialize in assessing the merits of each firm's theory. Their task is to assemble information, monitor performance, and evaluate the quality and likely future performance of the theories that managers propose, as these provide information to investors through earnings forecasts and buy and sell recommendations.

Unsurprisingly, managers' incentives to cultivate analyst coverage are substantial. All else being equal, more coverage positively influences the firm's valuation.[11] It does this by both reducing uncertainty for the investor and by functioning as a "marketing" arm for the security.[12] However, as the Monsanto story illustrates, just because these intermediaries shape the valuation of firms clearly does not mean they fully resolve the lemons problem. Indeed, the presence of analysts with such control may simply encourage managers to pander to analysts' preferences, which brings its own problems. Let's look at how that happens.

Obviously, sell-side analysts have incentives to dig in and effectively evaluate managers' strategies. Individual analysts are ranked on the accuracy of their forecasts and thus develop reputations with important financial implications. But there are other incentives in play as well. Brokerage firms, which employ the analysts, seek investment banking business from corporations as well as order flow from investors.

These incentives encourage analysts to be overly optimistic about the prospects of the firms they cover. While recent regulation has sought to eliminate these incentives, it has been less than fully effective, and it is hard to imagine how regulation could completely eliminate them. Suppose you are a respected analyst who attracts significant investment banking business. If your current employer will not reward you for this, a competitor will hire you away in hopes of attracting the investment banking business as well. The obvious result is that analysts are many times more likely to issue buy recommendations than sell recommendations. What's more, many brokerage firms will simply drop coverage rather than move to a sell recommendation, after which prospects for obtaining investment banking business from that company predictably diminish.

But there's another, less controversial factor at play. Analysts, like all individuals, seek to allocate their effort in ways that generate the best return on their time invested. Covering more firms expands order flow and reduces the costs spent per firm in analysis. But to economize on the effort expended per firm, and thereby cover more, analysts prefer firms that are easy to analyze—in other words, those pursuing theories that are familiar and simple.

The logical result, therefore, of choosing a more complex or unfamiliar strategy is a lemons discount or a costly-to-analyze discount not unlike that seen in used-car markets. While this all sounds fine in theory, is there any evidence to suggest it is empirically true?

The Monsanto report piqued my interest on this question, eventually leading to a large empirical study assessing whether indeed firms pursuing more complex or unfamiliar strategies receive a discount in capital markets.[13] Earlier studies had uncovered related empirical findings. MIT's Ezra Zuckerman, for example, found that firms tend to reshape themselves through divestitures and spinoffs to essentially "match" the "categories" covered by analysts.[14] Another study showed that net of other effects, analysts tend to avoid complex businesses with multiple operating divisions.[15]

My project with Lubomir Litov and Patrick Moreton focused on a topic even more central to the question. We examined the impact of a strategy's uniqueness on the level of coverage and the premium or discount that it received in capital markets.[16] We assumed that the most valuable corporate theories are built around uniqueness: either unique foresight about the value of a strategic bundle of assets, or the possession of unique assets that preclude others from enjoying similar value as they pursue complementary assets. We then examined all publicly traded firms from 1985 to 2007 and developed a measure of how unique a firm's strategy was relative to other firms in its primary industry.

Our study revealed several intriguing findings. First, we found that covering firms with more complex and unique strategies demands more effort from analysts. Analysts are able to cover fewer other firms when they cover a firm that is unique or complex. As a result, firms pursuing more complex and unusual strategies receive less analyst coverage, all else being equal. Second, we corroborated an abundance of earlier research showing that the amount of coverage matters to valuation (in other words, reduced coverage reduces valuation). Finally, we showed that firms pursuing more novel theories receive a valuation premium in the market consistent with the logic of chapter 1, but this premium is smaller than it might otherwise be because of the higher cost of coverage and lower resulting analyst coverage. The bottom line is that this uniqueness paradox is pervasive even in the market for publicly traded firms. Choosing unique theories, which may maximize long-term value, will likely receive a discount in the present.

How Should Managers Respond to the Lemons Problem?

In light of the lemons discount, firms face a dilemma in how to best pursue value creation. They can choose to pursue a unique corporate theory—one that they feel will ultimately maximize shareholder value, but will be discounted, possibly for a long period, due to the elevated cost of analysis, and that of course may turn out to be wrong. Or they can choose a theory that is inconsistent with their own beliefs about long-term value creation but that panders to the capital markets and is likely to generate a short- and even medium-term increase in market value, and that may even turn out to be right.

In the face of this dilemma, firms can make one of four choices:

COMPROMISE THE STRATEGIC THEORY. First, firms may choose to alter their theory in response to this lemons discount, instead adopting one that imposes a lesser information burden on analysts and enables more accurate analyst coverage. There is clear evidence that this approach works as predicted. One study finds that simplifying a firm's strategy through focus-increasing transactions increases both the volume and accuracy of analyst coverage.[17] Another finds evidence that managers do precisely this. They divest businesses to compose their strategy to better match the existing preferences of analysts.[18] However, this path may very well compromise the long-term potential for value creation.

THUMB YOUR NOSE AT THE MARKET. Second, companies may simply ignore what they believe is the market's shortsighted undervaluation and instead bank on the true value of their corporate theory eventually being revealed in superior operating returns. How feasible this option is depends on the patience of investors (and of course the accuracy of the manager's beliefs). Clearly, some investors are more willing than others to forgo current value increases for what may be higher future value. Hence, assembling investors who support the theory is a significant managerial task, regardless of whether the enterprise is an angel-funded new venture or a large multinational enterprise. Of course, if the theory proves accurate, investors' belief in it may provide tremendous value. As noted, capital markets are actually very much like the used-car market. If you, as an investor, find a trusted seller—a company with a valuable corporate theory, then the market affords real bargains.

INCREASE INFORMATION DISCLOSURE. Third, an organization can stay the course, but attempt to increase investors' access to information regarding its corporate theory. To do this, it may pursue one of several tactics. First, it can push analysts and investment banks to devote greater resources to analyzing the current strategy. For instance, the company may engage in aggressive publicity campaigns to market its theory to capital markets. Alternatively, it may choose to directly pay for analysis, an option that has become more possible in recent years with the emergence of "paid-for" analyst research firms that offer firms analyst coverage for a fee.[19] In recent years more than 35 percent of publicly traded firms received no security analyst coverage whatsoever, and as we have seen, the difference between having coverage and not having coverage on the market value of a firm is enormous.

TAKE THE COMPANY PRIVATE. Ultimately, neither assembling desired investors nor escalating information disclosure may prove sufficient. Casual evidence suggests that many managers pursuing more unique or complex strategies simply migrate to some form of private equity. We already know that funding new technology ventures is largely undertaken

by expert private investors because evaluating new technology is often too costly for public equity markets. The same
logic applies to the high information costs that accompany
evaluating the complex or unique theories of established corporations. Extensive empirical literature documents the dis-
appearance of conglomerates from public markets over the
past two decades but arguably conglomerates have merely
re-emerged as private equity firms, bundles of highly unrelated businesses, which are clearly very costly to analyze in
the composite. Going private creates proper incentives for
incurring the information costs required for accurate analysis and investment. While some suggest that private equity's primary benefit is solving the moral hazard problem with
high-powered incentives for managers, in my mind an equal,
if not greater benefit, is that it addresses the lemons problem.

Another way to go private is to find a large privately owned
acquirer. Koch Industries' recent purchase of pulp and paper
product giant Georgia-Pacific created the largest privately
owned company in the United States. As reported in the
Financial Times:

> [Georgia Pacific's assets] have underperformed the
> broader S&P500 index partly because it has an awk-
> ward mix of assets that are difficult to value together.
> Some of its consumer products, such as tissues, are
> in solid, high-margin niches that deserve a relatively
> high share-price multiple. Other activities, such as
> selling building products, are in volatile sectors where
> investors are beginning to worry about the effects of

a downturn in the US housing market . . . The combination means an otherwise strong company has been
trading at a significant discount to the sum of its parts
at a time when potential buyers have lots of cash and
borrowing is cheap.[20]

The logic is that by taking the company private, Georgia-
Pacific acquires patient investors who will allow managers to
play out their corporate theory and reveal its value. Moreover,
because Georgia-Pacific's complexity generated a discount,
Koch creates value through the deal. Thus, private equity—
whether in hedge funds or through privately owned groups—
finds underpriced assets not merely because the managers
were previously poorly motivated, but rather because the
capital markets were poorly informed about value. The clear
prediction of this logic, then, is that high-information-cost
strategies, including complex or unique strategies, will
migrate to private equity.

In the remainder of the book, I will assume that managers
are well-intentioned and seek to maximize long-term shareholder value. I will therefore not devote much attention
to how to optimize CEO governance in pursuit of the first
option by tying a manager's rewards ever more tightly to the
capital market's current assessment of firm value and investment opportunities.[21] Instead, I will turn my attention to
providing strategic guidance to managers who seek to apply
value-creating corporate theories. The first major implementation question is this: As you acquire complementary assets

and capabilities, how do you figure out whether you should purchase and control them or whether you should access them from suppliers through contracts? That is the focus of chapter 4.

LESSONS LEARNED

Managers face a fundamental dilemma in choosing strategic actions. Should they develop and faithfully adhere to their corporate theories of value creation or should they follow the signals of the financial markets? The explanation for the dilemma—and how to work through it, depends on which of two dynamics you believe to be dominant:

- **Moral hazard:** In this capital market perspective, often favored by investors, managers are hired to apply the knowledge and expertise they have to pursue shareholder interests, but may instead choose to pursue strategic paths that benefit them privately. The route to value-creation is one of making lazy, self-interested managers do what the market wants.

- **The lemons problem:** In this strategic perspective, often favored by managers, it is very difficult for markets to assess the value of original theories. Too often good theories get priced at the same level as the bad ones. The challenge is for well-intentioned managers to better communicate the value of their theories and thereby obtain the funds and patience required to pursue them.

All too often, the capital markets perspective dominates the strategic perspective, as market participants, including stock analysts, have insufficient incentive to dig in and accurately evaluate more unique and difficult to evaluate strategies. The upshot is that any value created by a good theory may well be discounted by the market. In this situation, managers have the following options:

- **Go along with the market:** This is often the easiest course and is likely, given incentive structures, to be the most personally remunerative course. But it amounts to giving up on genuine strategy making.

- **Communicate better:** This is easier said than done (else why would analysts avoid such strategies?), and in some settings disclosing the full details or even the logic of a strategy compromises its value by inviting competitive imitation.

- **Find the right shareholders:** In an increasing number of cases, management teams keen on applying real theories about how their firms create value have ended up taking companies private in some form rather than rely on the questionable strategic wisdom of the public markets.

PART TWO

Putting Value Together

CHAPTER 4

Make or Buy?

Whether to make or buy is one of the most notoriously difficult of strategic decisions.[1] While sustained value creation requires the constant expansion and modification of the firm, many of the assets and activities to which its corporate theory directs access are likely owned by others. Therefore, composing the value that your theory reveals demands sound decisions about when to acquire, configure, and own these assets (make) and when to merely contract for their outputs (buy).

There are vocal advocates, both in and out of the firm, for both paths. Open innovation gurus and outsourcing firms preach the near-universal virtue of outsourcing. Many voices within firms call for integration. All too often, our own intuition regarding make or buy decisions is terribly misguided. We integrate only to discover we should have outsourced and outsource only to discover we should have integrated. We see great value in keeping control of our assets and processes through integration, convinced we can outperform suppliers, only to discover our internal efforts are high-cost or low-quality. We see integration as an opportunity to capture suppliers' profits, only to discover that its price tag far exceeds its value. On the other hand, when we resist the temptation to integrate, we find that we have become massively dependent on a unique asset we don't possess and now pay dearly to access.

The wrong decisions can generate lost value of historically disastrous proportions. For example, forty years ago, the *Saturday Evening Post*'s demise was labeled "the greatest corporate disaster in American history."[2] At its peak, the *Post* had captured 30 percent of all magazine advertising in the United States. Its failure's proximate cause was a set of disastrous integration decisions. The CEO of the parent company, Curtis Publishing, was enamored of the control afforded by vertical integration, and he pursued it with a passion. He authorized the construction of a massive, state-of-the-art printing facility. He purchased three large paper mills to feed the presses. He acquired 262,000 acres of timberland to feed the mills. The firm also forward-integrated into circulation. The result was catastrophic, as internal assets quickly atrophied in cost performance or quality. Inevitably, the publisher collapsed.

Erroneous decisions to outsource can prove equally disastrous. IBM's 1984 introduction of the PC generated enormous value for customers. However, IBM also misjudged how to delineate the vertical boundaries of this business. It misguidedly followed a common, but frequently misleading, rubric derived from capabilities logic: out-source what you currently do poorly and remain integrated into what you do well.

If only the choice were that simple. While IBM correctly searched for and found capabilities it lacked outside the firm, the decision to outsource access to the operating system (DOS) and microprocessor (Intel's 8088) rather than acquire them ensured that most of the value created flowed to these suppliers. While IBM brilliantly assembled the assets and activities required to generate this enormous value, poor decisions about how to govern access to them fueled Microsoft and Intel's value growth rather than its own.

How do you avoid making mistakes like these? Assuming that a theory has revealed a clear idea of the assets and activities you want to combine and configure, doing this effectively requires decisions about what types of incentives are required for the people and organizations involved. Fundamentally, you must choose between two competing incentive systems, each with distinct advantages and disadvantages in the behaviors they motivate. Naturally, the best-case scenario is you can successfully minimize the inherent trade-offs in choosing one or the other and instead enjoy the "best of both worlds." But these tradeoffs do exist and this difficult choice between outsourcing and integrating remains. Understanding the precise nature of the trade-offs inherent in each is critical to creating and then capturing the value envisioned in the theory. Let's look at the pros and cons of each approach.

The Marvel of the Market

As Friedrich Hayek described, markets induce "individuals to do . . . desirable things without having anyone tell them what to do."[3] Such motivation or control, when well matched to needs, is miraculous and without substitute. In this ideal state, with little effort on your part, the markets that surround your firm powerfully motivate a host of actors to generate products and services tailored to your needs. Markets engage suppliers in the cognitive task of discovering products and services that complement your assets and activities. They motivate suppliers to constantly reduce costs and enhance the value they offer you, ultimately embedding their unique knowledge into products and services that solve your problems.

Contracts may also shape incentives in these markets, promoting in particular commitment to longer-term exchange. Yet with contracts, even long-term contracts, suppliers remain constantly aware of your option to switch, which gives them strong incentives to increase the value they provide, stay abreast of relevant new technology, and consistently drive down costs. Equally important are the strong incentives for other suppliers to lure your business by enhancing the value they offer or to underprice your current supplier.

A decision to outsource therefore reflects confidence in the wisdom and creativity of outside economic actors—a belief that these outside actors will be strongly motivated to create solutions superior in cost or quality to what you can build. In this sense, the choice to outsource is a nod to humility over hubris—a recognition of the market's frequent capacity to motivate and control better than you can. It was this eventual recognition that drove big pharma firms to increasingly outsource R&D or early-stage drug research through market contracts. For such an activity, market control is tremendously effective. Decisions to shut out the market's individual and collective wisdom by integrating an activity should therefore be made only after particularly careful review. Such decisions demand confidence that your capacity to direct others' assets and activities is truly superior to the motivation that market prices provide to these external actors.

When markets fail

If markets succeed by inducing actors to elevate your firm's value, they fail when the they induce behaviors different from the ones you seek *and* when the contracting costs to reshape these behaviors are excessive. When such divergence occurs, the choice between make and buy requires a conceptually simple comparison: How do the costs of shaping the desired incentives and behaviors through contracts compare to the costs of doing so through integration? The strategic manager then can select the less costly of the two. But although conceptually elegant, the calculation required to compare these costs is challenging: it requires forecasting the implications of future behaviors about which there is enormous uncertainty. The cost of using the market or contracts to reshape incentives increases sharply when your theory about the optimal path to value creation, and specifically the use of others' assets and resources, diverges from others' beliefs about their optimal use. The cost of using the market also increases when outsourcing enables suppliers to potentially capture a substantial portion of the value that your theory creates—a problem often called *holdup* (discussed in more detail below). These elevated costs of shaping incentives through markets typically occur when value creation requires complex coordination; unique, firm specific investments; and some uncertainty about the outcome.

One of the first challenges is convincing others that yours is the optimal path to value creation. This is particularly difficult when your proposed path to value creation demands investments in activities and assets that your suppliers fail to see as value maximizing. This most often arises when the investments you propose are specific or unique to your firm and your proposal for value creation, but useless (or substantially less useful) elsewhere. Suppose you want a manufacturer to construct a unique production facility tailored to your needs, or you seek an IT firm that will embed itself in your firm, learn your ways, and craft customized software applications. Putting together a contract to generate such investments may be extraordinarily costly, since specifying the configuration of assets and activities you want may be difficult. However, the real challenge is that suppliers will seek guaranteed future returns to make these investments, and such guarantees are almost impossible to make, given the uncertainty about what the future holds and the value the investments will generate.

The second challenge in attracting these specific investments is the perceived threat of a holdup (see "The Holdup Problem"). The supplier fears that if it makes the specific investments you require, you will be able to demand more favorable contract terms, regardless of what the original

The Holdup Problem

My first exposure to the holdup problem was part of freshman writing class on the topic of Leland Stanford and the railroad. My research project described an extreme version of the classic holdup problem. In 1869, Southern Pacific Railroad announced it would lay tracks through California's central valley along a designated path. Southern Pacific invited settlers to begin developing the land adjacent to this path, suggesting that the price would be "$2.50 per acre and up," promising that any improvements to the land would not be factored into the final price, but also stipulating that the final price would be set and payment would occur after the tracks were laid. Years later, with settlers' investments in the land well in place, investments that were largely immovable and thus highly specific to the adjacent railroad tracks, the Southern Pacific set the price of the land at $35 per acre. Settlers were outraged. The result was a bitter dispute between settlers and the railroad that erupted in Tulare County, California, into a gunfight and massacre of both railroad men and settlers. Such is a classic holdup—a problem that arises frequently in business exchanges.

contract specified. More precisely, you are now in a position to hold the supplier up for the value of the unique portion of its investment—the portion unusable elsewhere.[4] For instance, you can insist on lowering the prices you pay for the asset, and with no other purchaser for it, acceding to your renegotiated terms may be the supplier's best option. Foresighted suppliers will refuse to make such investments in the first place without safeguards against this possible holdup. And the costs of a contract that will induce a supplier to invest in unique assets may be very high.

Unfortunately, if suppliers do become providers of a critical and unique component of a product that proves valuable in the marketplace, then your contracting problem may be even worse. Now you have a new dilemma—a supplier with a powerful claim on the value you envisioned—basically in a position to hold *you* up and appropriate a substantial portion of the value of your created asset. In this sense, the holdup problem that elevates contracting costs and fuels market failure is often both symmetric and fully dynamic. Sometimes clever contracting and a trusting relationship are sufficient to overcome these challenges. Frequently, they are not.

To illustrate, in the late 1990s, Pixar willingly invested in animated films that were highly dependent on Disney's marketing engine for success. As Pixar developed its unrivaled talent in computer-generated animation, it became an enormously valuable and unique complement to Disney's other assets. Because no other animator was in a position to generate the same value for Disney, Pixar held joint claim to a tremendous amount of Disney's value and was therefore armed with a clear holdup threat. At the same time, the threat was somewhat symmetric. Disney was also a unique comple-ment to Pixar. The magnitude of the codependence and the complexity of the required coordination rendered contract negotiations extremely contentious and costly, ultimately leading to the contract's expiration without renewal. Disney eventually purchased Pixar in 2006 for a price of $7.4 billion— a price that reveals the magnitude of this unique comple-mentarity and Pixar's holdup threat. Whether that price still left value for Disney to capture remains a debate for business school courses. What is unambiguous, however, is that Dis-ney erred in not maintaining a state-of-the-art animation studio of its own—an asset central to its corporate theory— and in allowing its internal skills in animation to atrophy.

Holdup risks can also arise even when there is no need for investment. An envisioned path to value creation may involve little more than a novel combination of assets and activities in their present form. For instance, the IBM PC business model required suppliers to make very few investments spe-cific to IBM or the IBM PC. For example, the core element of the hardware platform—Intel's 1088 microprocessor—while unique and difficult for others to replicate, was a stock item that required no additional development. However, once demand for PCs skyrocketed, revealing their value—an outcome that was considered a near certainty from the beginning—Intel suddenly possessed a unique complemen-tary input and was therefore positioned to capture a large portion of the resulting value. While Microsoft's contribution required marginally greater investments specific to the PC, IBM's failure to integrate ensured that Microsoft owned a unique complement to the PC and was thus able to capture enormous value as well. In contrast, IBM's marketing and sales engine, while an initially important complement in propelling the PC to a de facto industry standard, became both less valuable and widely available once that standard was established.

In summary, markets and contracts fail to provide the necessary incentives when the configuration of assets and activities you need differs from the configurations that suppliers are motivated to build, or when suppliers' customization of the assets you seek positions them to appropriate all of the value. These differences arise particularly when creating value involves assets or activities that are uniquely complementary to your firm. Whenever suppliers are in possession of such assets, they are positioned to appropriate much of the resulting value. Attempting to solve this problem with market contracts is exceptionally costly and difficult and becomes a primary motivation for integration.

The Integration Advantage

While the markets can powerfully shape supplier behavior without a deliberate effort to bring this about, integration provides a solution when market incentives, even shaped by contracts, fail to generate the behaviors a firm needs, or fail to do so efficiently. As D. H. Robertson suggests, firms are "islands of conscious power in [an] ocean of unconscious cooperation."[5] Sometimes integration's control is simply essential.

At the most basic level, integration allows you to coordinate value-creating assets and activities without having to persuade others of the superiority of your vision or the value of investing in it. Investments that come from within the firm also do not pose a holdup risk that an outside supplier will appropriate all of the value you jointly create.

Smith & Wesson's recent decision to acquire Tri Town Precision Plastics, its key supplier of custom injection molding, seems to reflect this logic. Before the purchase, two-thirds of Tri Town's output went to Smith & Wesson. But Smith & Wesson likely worried that Tri Town was reluctant to make any further investments specific to Smith & Wesson, fearing holdup and instead looking to find other customers that could decrease its dependence on Smith & Wesson. By taking ownership of Tri Town's assets, Smith & Wesson eliminated any disincentives to make these specific investments and thereby skirted the holdup problem. Smith & Wesson now has an internal supplier with every reason to pursue its vision, including the asset needs to fulfill that vision.

Although integration converts motivated market actors into arguably less motivated employees, it can compensate for this through the formation of cooperative norms that may promote the knowledge sharing and coordination required to effectively pursue a corporate theory. What's required is skillful leadership that leverages enhanced incentives to cooperate (people are now rewarded for furthering the acquirer's goal rather than their previous one) to facilitate a shared commitment to the firm's theory.

The control trap

It is essential to remember, however, that with make or buy decisions, it nearly always makes sense to outsource and rely on market incentives unless there is a real need for complex coordination or specific investments. Discerning when and where such conditions truly exist is therefore central to getting governance right. The problem is that some firms and managers have an insatiable appetite for control that translates into a strong bias toward integration, even when these conditions do not hold. Often, this bias reflects their hubris—a conviction that their control is superior to others' in generating value. More frequently, it reflects a misguided belief that integration affords access to all of its virtues with little cost. In other words, managers discount the market's *unique* capacity to powerfully motivate "unconscious cooperation." But this thinking is deeply flawed, since in almost all circumstances, the cost of integration's control is the loss of the market's motivation.[6]

Firms have made this mistake repeatedly. For years, big pharma companies acquired small biotech firms to gain access to their cutting-edge research and exceptional talent, only to discover post integration that the powerful incentives the market had previously provided to key talent inside these biotech firms could not be maintained after integration. Accordingly, key talent walked and productivity plummeted.

Large oil and gas companies confronted a similar outcome in integrating small, highly effective exploration outfits. These acquirers similarly struggled post integration to replicate the market incentives that had driven the independent exploration operations, and were unable to effectively either retain talent or motivate effective exploration. After many painful lessons, both big pharma and big oil shifted toward relying on outsourcing for these activities.

But this does beg an interesting question: Why can't firms simply replicate market incentives inside the firm and avoid this compromise? That way they can have their cake and eat it too.

An Either-Or Choice

There are inherent impediments to firms' attempts to replicate internally the market's strong incentives. Inside firms, employees constantly compare rewards and envy those receiving higher pay. They particularly assess the equity of what they observe, and all too frequently conclude that the pay awarded to high performers, especially the lavish performance-based incentives, is unfair. We know from longstanding research in organizational behavior that when employees perceive that they are receiving inequitable treatment, they reduce their efforts, lobby for more pay, or simply leave—behaviors very costly for the firm.[7]

To illustrate the impediments to replicating market incentives, consider Harvard's efforts to manage its massive

$36 billion endowment. To motivate the employees who managed various classes of funds within the portfolio, Harvard devised incentives that replicated market incentives—the types of financial rewards that would be received by fund managers who would receive Harvard's business if Harvard outsourced the activity. The resulting performance was spectacular, with returns that far exceeded benchmark investment funds by asset managers elsewhere—in several cases, returns that were double those earned by benchmark comparisons. In fact, the performance was so spectacular and the reward structure sufficiently market-like that several of these Harvard employees earned as much as $25–$30 million a year in performance bonuses.

Faculty, students, parents, and alumni, however, were outraged when these salaries were disclosed. Larry Summers, Harvard's president at the time, defended the system by noting that generating this type of performance using external fund managers would cost even more, which was likely quite true. However, as the complaints and resulting costs mounted, Harvard flattened the compensation. Predictably, the key fund managers departed, leaving Harvard to take the rational next step. It outsourced key portions of its portfolio management to, not surprisingly, these same fund managers, now employed elsewhere. Note that the incentives themselves were quite effective in generating the high performance of employees. The impediment was the cost of these incentives to the university—the costs imposed by social comparison.

Performance-based incentives, while easily designed and available through market contracts, are difficult and costly to replicate within the firm, giving markets a unique advantage in generating motivation and initiative among a wide range of talent. Within the boundaries of the firm, perceptions of inequity in response to performance-based incentives, like those observed in faculty, alumni, and students at Harvard, impose costs that are directly borne by the firm. When such services and incentives are deployed outside a firm in market contracts, the firm is largely immune to these costs. While employees may envy the pay of those outside the firm, such envy is less likely to generate politicking for change, reduced effort, or outright sabotage of others' efforts.[8] Thus, as Harvard's treasurer, Ronald Daniel, commented during the height of the uproar: " . . . if the activity was outsourced, you wouldn't care."[9] He was entirely correct. Because individuals care tremendously when lucrative incentives generate high pay for colleagues inside the firm, social comparison constrains the capacity of firms to effectively replicate markets. This then leaves them with a choice between accessing the virtues of markets or the virtues of integration, but not both.

How to Manage the Choice Over Time

Although one choice usually precludes the other at the time the decision is made, managers need to remember that make or buy choices need not be static. Decisions to integrate or outsource continue to shape behaviors, investments, and actions. Outsourcing consistently fuels strong supplier incentives to lower costs and generate innovative solutions, but provides ongoing weak incentives for them to supply valuable firm-specific investments that the firm may want. Integration supports complex coordination and specialized investments, but provides weaker incentives to lower costs and generate innovation. Because more often than not the advantages of both are needed at some point, choices to make or buy often sow the seeds of their own destruction. For an outsourced asset or activity, the passage of time may reveal diminishing returns to market incentives, but increasing returns to firm-specific investments or complex coordination. For an integrated activity, time may reveal the reverse—diminishing returns to the specific investments or complex coordination that integration provides, and increasing returns to the innovation or cost reduction that market incentives fuel.

Not infrequently, firms vacillate between make or buy choices over time. The IT function is a particularly common candidate and the dynamics are illustrative. When an IT function is integrated, it has incentives to generate customized solutions and service for internal clients. However, these same incentives, which motivate firm-specific learning and customization, also provide little reward for efforts to remain technologically current or to drive down costs and elevate value. By contrast, when outsourced, the IT function is strongly motivated to lower costs and remain technologically current, but incentives to invest in highly customized solutions are weak. With the passage of time, the incremental benefits of the current choice may diminish, while the forgone benefits of the alternative choice increase. Consequently, yesterday's decision to integrate may directly lead to tomorrow's decision to outsource. These dynamic patterns reflect the inherent advantages and flaws in both make and buy and their mutual incompatibility.

LESSONS LEARNED

Make or buy decisions are not mere items on a checklist— once done, never to be revisited. Instead, these decisions need frequent review, with a recognition that a decision to switch is not a signal of failure. Rather, it reflects the passage of time and a growing imbalance in the advantages and disadvantages of the original choice.

It's also not enough to have a sound theory guiding your efforts to assemble combinations of assets and activities. You need to make strategic decisions around how you will manage access to these activities and assets: should you own an asset or should you access it through a market contract. The costs and benefits of each are:

- **Markets:** These provide powerful performance incentives, but if the incentives are not aligned with your interests, you can become a hostage to powerful suppliers or fail to obtain specific investments that you need suppliers to make. You may also suffer if value creation requires coordination of knowledge or operations because market mechanisms may not promote the type of sharing you demand.

- **Integration:** Ownership makes knowledge and asset sharing easier, guarantees appropriate investments, and by definition grants you control of the asset. But unless these are important, owning assets and resources will fail because integration usually cannot offer the rewards and incentives for performance that can be obtained through market mechanisms.

To recap: The cost-benefit balance is not static and smart organizations will review their decisions to integrate or out-source assets and capabilities as their needs evolve.

CHAPTER 5

Shaping External
Relationships

As shown in chapter 4, many of the assets and resources that a company will need to obtain to put its theory into practice are best left outside the firm and sourced through market relationships. But there are many types of market relationships, and a central question in pursuing a particular strategic experiment is which to pursue; for example, whether to purchase the inputs from the lowest-cost supplier or develop a relationship with a few favored ones. Answering that question is a perennial challenge, with wide ranging options that continue to unfold. As Friedrich Hayek commented, "[while] man has learned to use [the market] . . . , he is still very far from having learned to make the best use of it."[1] Of course, much has changed in the seventy years since Hayek made that statement. We'll begin by understanding how theory and best practices have evolved before offering guidance on how to confront the challenge of composing sup-plier relationships.

An Invasion of Alliances

Japan's economic expansion in the late 1970s and 1980s was remarkable. For many in the United States, it felt like an inva-sion, as Japanese firms captured substantial market share in highly visible markets such as consumer electronics, semi-conductors, and automobiles.

Japan's success was most visible in the automotive indus-try. In California, the share of Japanese cars on California roads exploded. This success was pinned to a remarkable manufacturing system that seemed to deliver both higher quality and lower cost. Academics, consultants, and indi-vidual firms all scrambled to uncover the secret. By most accounts, including that of Japan's own Ministry of Interna-tional Trade and Industry (MITI), the central feature was a remarkably different approach to managing buyer-supplier relationships.[2]

The novelty of this approach was most apparent when it was contrasted with the practice of US manufacturing firms. Most of these, at the time, acquired parts and components in one of two distinct ways: through outright integration or through arm's-length contracting. In sourcing parts and components, both GM and Ford were substantially inte-grated. The remaining parts and components were sourced through contracts with outside vendors that were rebid each year to ensure suppliers were disciplined on cost. Accordingly, US automakers maintained a robust set of alternative suppliers for each part.

The Japanese approach could not have been more different. To begin with, Japanese automakers were considerably less integrated, deriving only a small fraction of their parts and components from internal sources. More importantly, the much broader set of assets that Japanese firms acquired through outsourcing was managed in an entirely different manner. The Japanese maintained long-term, stable relations with a small set of suppliers. Rather than using a system of one-year contracts with annual rebidding and robust competition, the Japanese adopted four-to-five-year contracts and worked collaboratively with suppliers to both innovate and reduce costs. Moreover, while these contracts had official four-to-five-year terms, implicitly they were of far longer duration, essentially without termination dates. While the Japanese by no means invented collaborative relationships, they powerfully demonstrated the potential to generate competitive advantage from them.

The behaviors of suppliers operating within these competing models could also not have been more different. Japanese suppliers made extensive investments that were quite specific to their buyers. They worked collaboratively with automakers to develop and design innovative parts and to foster efficient manufacturing practices. US suppliers behaved very differently. With a one-year time horizon and a decision process based almost entirely around bid prices, suppliers had very weak incentives to make customized, cost-reducing

119

production investments, let alone long-term investments in innovative designs. Moreover, to manage the constant churn in suppliers, US automobile firms maintained a cast of thousands to manage the procurement and contracting process. In the mid-1980s, GM purportedly had a procurement staff that was ten times larger than Toyota's, though it produced only twice as many cars.[3]

Given US automakers' high-cost procurement operation and, more importantly, the relatively poor outcomes from procurement, their aggressive degree of integration is not surprising. But look at the very different outcome of the Japanese model. The greater efficiency inherent in the Japanese approach to contracting and the far more impressive outputs, especially in using suppliers to generate innovation, enabled the Japanese automakers to be far less integrated. While this approach to buyer-supplier relations was particularly evident in automobiles, Japanese firms used the same approach in other industries as well.

US firms responded predictably. During the late 1980s and early '90s, they aggressively set about reconfiguring their supply arrangements to more closely resemble the Japanese. Firms dramatically reduced the number of suppliers with which they engaged—one study showed that for US automobiles introduced before 1986, the average US automaker maintained 4.75 suppliers per part, but for models introduced after 1986, that number dropped to 1.42 suppliers per part—essentially identical to the average for the big three Japanese automakers.[4] A similarly dramatic shift occurred in contract length. While corresponding measureable statistics do not match those of Japanese relationships, the shifts speak to the clear intent of US firms to develop more close collaborative relationships with fewer suppliers.

This trend was not restricted to the auto industry. Firms in nearly all industries began to develop more collaborative arrangements with their outside suppliers. One representative study calculated that the portion of business conducted through alliances jumped from 5 percent in 1990 to 40 percent by 2010.[5] While some of this shift is likely simple reclassification, it certainly highlights the magnitude of the change. Consultants and academics helped fuel the movement, promoting alliance capitalism and encouraging firms to compose a relational advantage.[6] Consultants advocated that US firms form their own *keiretsu* (the Japanese term for networks of close supply relations) and engage in extensive relationship building with suppliers.

Alliances also became a standard vehicle for managing innovation and R&D in a wide range of industries outside the manufacturing sector. Within pharmaceuticals, for instance, R&D alliances between research-oriented biotech firms and big pharma became standard and a critical vehicle for survival.

For many firms, the formation of alliances naturally led to a trend toward vertical disintegration as the advantages of outsourcing became stronger. However, just as the path to efficiently managing external supply relations seemed entirely clear, the late 1990s ushered in a revolution in information technology that arguably prompted an even more dramatic wave of change—one that illuminated a whole new array of options in efficiently managing external relations.

The IT Revolution

In 2000, there were 361 million internet users. By 2010, that number was nearly 2 billion, and by 2014, it exceeded 3.3 billion.[7] During the 1990s, corporate investment in information technology increased at the remarkable rate of 24 percent per year.[8] These investments, coupled with burgeoning internet use, enabled more robust communication, monitoring, and coordination with suppliers and in the process again reshaped how firms manage their relationships with external providers and suppliers.

While these investments provided important support to collaborative long-term alliances, their most visible influence has been in reshaping arm's-length relationships with suppliers and other outside providers. For instance, many firms have accessed or developed electronic procurement auctions. In these auctions, the buyer digitally broadcasts a detailed RFQ (request for quotation) for a bundle of related parts or services that it wants to contract for. Suppliers signal their interest, and the buyer screens candidates on prior performance, technological capability, equipment, location, or other criteria, and invites some to electronically submit bids (the buyer often has a stable of prequalified suppliers who can also bid without going through the review process). Not all interested suppliers are invited to bid, as the participation of low-quality suppliers will dampen the interest of high-quality suppliers, as they fear being low-balled. Typically, the invited suppliers can submit multiple bids during the appointed time window in response to other bids. At the conclusion of the bid event, the buyer approves a bid (not necessarily the lowest) and enters into a supply contract.[9]

The advantage of these auctions is the potential they offer for buyers to discover new suppliers with new capabilities and cost positions.[10] Such broad reach is particularly important in an environment of changing technology, where tomorrow's optimal exchange may differ from today's. A buyer's broad access to new suppliers also pushes existing suppliers to remain up-to-date and price competitive. Organizations ranging from large manufacturers, such as Emerson, General Electric, and Caterpillar to the US federal government make extensive use of electronically enabled procurement to both streamline and extend their supply relations and elevate their bargaining power. These auctions are either self-managed, or managed by third-party providers such as Ariba or FedBid.

IT has also profoundly shaped how firms engage others in innovation. One of the real revolutions in procurement broadly is the growing use of parties outside the firm not merely as a source of production or distribution, but as vehicles to solve innovation problems and challenges or to design and develop the products you sell. However, the outside access is not garnered through alliances but arm's-length relationships with distant sources of knowledge—not suppliers with whom firms have a deeply embedded relationship, but those completely unknown to them.

One of the rallying cries of the broad movement toward more open innovation is the belief, first articulated by Bill Joy at Sun Microsystems, that "most of the smartest people work for someone else." In other words, those with the simplest, most effective, and least costly solutions to the problems firms seek to solve are likely to work elsewhere. And, most likely firms have no idea where they work—no idea where this critical knowledge resides. Entering into an alliance with a known provider may prove vastly inferior to inviting a crowd of potential providers to offer their solutions or proposals. IT provides remarkable vehicles for doing precisely this, enabling firms to develop or utilize creative ways to engage others.

Procter & Gamble's post-2000 experience provides a wonderful illustration of a firm that has used IT to radically reshape its approach to organizing innovation. For decades, P&G invested heavily in developing internal R&D labs and strong technical talent as its source for innovation. However, flattening sales and the declining success of new products caused a sudden and significant drop in the company's market value. CEO AG Lafley, having observed that in consumer products as with so many other industries, small firms or even independent inventors are the primary source of breakthrough innovation, determined to completely revamp P&G's approach to innovation. The key question for P&G therefore became: *How do you design an organizational model that efficiently accesses the vast innovative talent outside the company?*

Simply hiring inventors individually or acquiring the small firms that employed them was not really an option. The company had no real idea of who employed these valuable inventors or where they could find them. What's more, P&G recognized the risks inherent in integration discussed in chapter 4—that acquiring small, innovative firms would likely crush their innovativeness or that the individuals P&G particularly valued might leave. The goal instead was to generate productive connections with these previously unknown external sources—and the way to achieve it was to transform the seventy-five hundred researchers inside P&G, who historically abhorred anything "not invented here," into researchers actively seeking connections to the hundreds of thousands of researchers and inventors outside the firm working on relevant related technology.

IT was the primary vehicle fueling these connections. Researchers used the web to scour the scientific literature and patent databases. P&G established proprietary networks with its top suppliers that facilitated posting and sharing technology briefs to which the suppliers privately responded. From this electronic prospecting with existing suppliers, new collaboratively staffed R&D projects were created. More importantly, in an effort to access the vast wealth of technologies and competencies unknown to internal researchers, P&G also aggressively participated in third-party innovation platforms such as Innocentive, NineSigma, and YourEncore. These platforms specialize in distributing particular types of problems and challenges and in providing access to differing crowds of problem solvers.

The effort was remarkably successful. A wealth of new, unique, and highly effective connections that fueled innovation emerged. R&D productivity increased 60 percent, while R&D investment decreased. Success with new product innovations also doubled, with a host of new products ranging from Pringles Prints to the Magic Eraser born from this effort.

Of course, there is nothing particularly new about using outsiders to innovate. Contracting out external research, licensing technology, and accessing user communities have long been central to generating innovation across many industries.[11] But what has clearly changed at P&G and elsewhere is the use of technology to facilitate collaboration, design, and development across distance. Moreover, platforms that support crowdsourced innovation have become both more accessible and effective. In addition to those accessed by P&G, many other platforms facilitate efficiently posting problems to solve and accessing problem solvers. Many specialize in devising competitions that engage the crowd in problem solving through active online communities. As discussed by Kevin Boudreau and Karim Lakhani in a 2013 *Harvard Business Review* article, many of the contest platforms, such as as Kaggle, TopCoder, Tongal, HYVE, Quirky, crowdSPRING, DesignCrowd have become highly specialized in solving particular types of problems (e.g. advertising, software programming, product design) and therefore in attracting specialized problem-solving communities.[12]

An Embarrassment of Choices

Just as getting the make or buy choice right is essential to creating the value your theory envisions, so too is correctly

choosing how to access what you buy. Here too the answer is
not a simple one. A substantial shift toward more alliance-like
relations has fueled dramatic performance improvements in
a wide range of industries. An entirely different approach, fed
by more aggressive use of arm's-length auctions and crowdsourcing innovation, has fueled performance improvements
in others.

In sum, the past three decades have been a period of
remarkable innovation in sourcing, leading many firms in
very different directions—directions that have often changed
with time. Some firms have sought to construct collaborative
supply relationships with deeply embedded social connections, perhaps in the process pushing outside the firm many
exchanges that were previously within the firm. Other firms
have aggressively shifted to expanding their use of technology-
assisted markets, contests, and innovation platforms that
have either transformed relationships previously managed
through alliances into more arm's-length exchanges, or have
pushed previously internal exchanges outside the firm. The
use of alliances, as formally recorded in various databases,
appears to have peaked in the mid-to-late 1990s. The use of
electronically assisted exchanges ballooned from that point
on. Today, many firms use a unique combination of these
alternatives.

Given the vast array of alternatives, with no shortage of
advocates for each, what should guide your firm's path? When
are the deeply embedded social relationships characteristic
of long-term alliances the best choice for creating the value
that you envision? When are the deliberately arm's-length

auctions, contests, and innovation platforms a better option? At the most basic level, the answer to this question is similar to the one for make or buy choices: the choice hinges on the value of relationships in delivering what your theory envisions relative to the value that the market's capacity to broadly search and invite brings to realizing that vision.

For any given exchange both alliances and arm's-length arrangements are likely to have merits. Identifying an ideal exchange partner is indispensable, but so is some measure of cooperation and exchange-specific investment. But again, as with make or buy, the two paths are somewhat contradictory. Alliances encourage suppliers to make exchange-specific investments and generally facilitate trust and cooperative exchange, but they can also breed complacency and curtail a firm's capacity to broadly search and discover new valuable exchanges. Arm's-length procurement through RFQs, auctions, contests, and platforms invite and promote broad searches that induce those with valuable capabilities, knowledge, and capabilities to self-identify, but may also discourage the type of specialized investment you might need. Going too far in either direction undermines performance. The auto industry's obsession with competitive bidding and arm's-length auctions led to dramatic underperformance relative to their emerging peers from Japan. Alliances proved the remedy. P&G's focus on integration and a narrow set of external exchange relations stifled its potential for innovation. Broadcast searches and tapping into markets and crowds proved the solution. Getting this governance choice right is critical to delivering the value your corporate theory envisions.

Making the Right Call

Decisions about the composition of external relationships should be shaped by the attributes of the problem you seek to solve or the attributes of the envisioned exchange. While there is a wide range of potential attributes, only three are essential to defining the scope of control required by a particular exchange. I discuss these below in the form of three key questions. Note that these questions and therefore the prescribed approach are specific to a particular exchange or problem; they do not define a general company policy. Firms effective in external procurement will have large portfolios of paths to procurement, ranging from collaborative alliances and partnerships to arm's-length procurement auctions and crowdsourcing.

Who possesses the knowledge critical to constructing the value you envision?

The central question in determining how to shape relationships with external parties is determining whether you or they possess the knowledge critical to managing their actions and behaviors in a way that creates the value you foresee.

If you don't have the right knowledge, assuming undeserved control and influence over suppliers through an alliance and/or an elaborate contract carries a clear cost. It reduces the motivation of external parties who may have a much better sense of how to optimally use their assets, products, and technology than you do. And importantly, your commitment to an alliance may discourage other potential providers of the solutions or assets you require—and the knowledge required to effectively use them—from self-identifying. As I have previously noted, markets have the almost-magical power to motivate others to do what is desirable without your having to direct or control them. In a profoundly insightful comment, Friedrich Hayek remarked that "the most significant fact about this system [the market] is the economy of knowledge in which it operates, or how little the individual participants need to know [about other actors] in order to be able to take the right action."[13] A course of action that might cut you off from this rich resource should be pursued with the greatest of caution.

Clearly, in situations where the only critical knowledge you need to reveal may be a description of the part you want manufactured or the problem you want to solve, a market with arm's-length relationships offers the best solution, prompting suppliers possessing valuable low-cost solutions to aggressively bid for your business and demanding very little in the way of your control.

But in situations where your ongoing direction and knowledge is vital to shaping the actions of the external provider, a long-term collaborative alliance may be needed. These situations are most likely to arise when your expectations of your supplier's value-maximizing actions, investments, or behaviors differs from theirs, meaning that you would need carefully crafted contracts and extensive monitoring for a market-based collaboration to work. In these settings, therefore, convincing providers to deviate from the behaviors that market incentives prompt will very likely require the greater control that an alliance enables.

How unique is the solution you seek?

In chapter 4, I discussed at some length the problem of holdup that arises when the nature of an exchange demands that you and/or the supplier make unique investments that are specific to the exchange relationship. As noted, suppliers, recognizing little alternative use for these investments, are reluctant to make them in the first place, as they see no outlet to monetize them if the relationship is terminated, or even if you threaten to do so. At the same time, you may face precisely the same dilemma. You may be unwilling to invest in the exchange fearing the external provider may terminate or threaten to terminate the relationship and thereby hold you up for the value of your specific investments.

Continuity, trust, and cooperation, therefore, are critical when your assets and activities and your supplier's assets and activities are already unique, or through investment will become specific or uniquely complementary. Without integration, only continuity and trust in the exchange will motivate both you and the supplier to make the specialized investments needed for the exchange. Absent any expectations of longevity and trust, both parties are wary of losing the potential value in these specific investments—value that only emerges through extended exchange. Your task in these circumstances is to build collaborative exchange relations that promote trust and cooperation.

By contrast, when multiple suppliers can provide your firm with the value you seek, or when changes in underlying technology mean that the optimal supplier changes over time, then continuity in supply relationships offers little value. Under these conditions, engaging a multitude of potential exchange partners in efforts to win your business far exceeds any value in the greater trust that accompanies continuity in exchange. Here, a capacity to easily shift suppliers without any social obligations or commitments is critical to sustained value creation.

How difficult is it to prescribe or measure the behaviors or outcomes you want?

It is difficult to motivate through markets and contracts what you cannot specify and measure. But frequently, value creation demands complex coordination of activities of a form difficult to map out in advance. Instead, ongoing adaptation is essential. Value creation may also demand extensive knowledge sharing as you and an external partner work to create something valuable and novel. Since the exact composition of this configuration is unknown in advance, specifying the ideal behaviors or outcomes is impossible. Here your objective is to extensively share knowledge and in real time orchestrate this entirely novel recombination.

While a corporate theory may help identify a manufacturer or a technology provider with whom to exchange, it may reveal few specifics about what you seek. This inability to precisely define the course of action places value on building a collaborative alliance. In fact, an arm's-length market exchange is likely to exacerbate the coordination problem, discouraging both the knowledge sharing and careful coordination required. Problems that are highly complex and involve the melding of vast amounts of knowledge from disparate sources are likely to call for either outright integration or close collaborative alliances. On the other hand, if you can precisely define a problem you need solved or a product, service, or part you need provided, then devices like an arm's-length exchange, an electronic procurement auction, or even a contest may prove sufficient.

In summary, three factors drive your choice in locating exchanges along the spectrum from collaborative alliances to arm's-length exchanges: (1) the importance of the knowledge you possess relative to knowledge your supplier possesses in shaping supplier actions and behavior, (2) the uniqueness of the investments required, and (3) the difficulty in measuring or prescribing desired behaviors. Where suppliers have the knowledge critical to solving your problems and effectively satisfying the exchange, when little specific investment is required, and when desired outcomes are measurable, then contracts, auctions, contests, and crowdsourcing may be the best choice. When these conditions don't hold, developing close, long-term relationships may prove the key to success ("Why Contracts Matter" expands the role of contracts in developing these long-term relationships).

Why Contracts Matter

The precise nature of a contract's influence is the subject of some dispute. A study from the 1960s, still widely cited, claims that "detailed negotiated contracts can get in the way of creating good exchange relationships between business units."[a] The study argues that contracts signal a lack of trust and turn what would otherwise be a "cooperative venture into an antagonistic horse-trade." Others have also posited that legal remedies erode interpersonal relationships and replace "an individual's 'good will' with objective formal requirements."[b] These scholars point to the fact that in collaborative exchanges, contracts are largely ignored by both parties, arguing further that the formality of a contract crowds out good behavior.

Yet empirical studies on the role played by contracts in shaping cooperative relationships suggest that these experts have the argument backward. While there are certainly pockets of the global economy that effectively enjoy collaborative relationships without formal contracts, the evidence suggests that well-crafted contracts play an important and positive role in promoting the formation of collaborative exchange and encouraging trust.[c] Nobel Prize winner Douglass North suggests that formal institutions such as contracts serve as complements in providing informal control.[d] Formal contracts extend the expected duration of a relationship. With a longer exchange horizon, suppliers are simply more likely to cooperate, enabling closer coordination and facilitating specific investments. Contracts may also specify procedures for flexibly adapting relationships, which supports the longevity of association. In this sense, well-crafted contracts and collaborative alliances are complements rather than substitutes.

Thus, the key to developing valuable supplier relationships is more than meals and golf. Rather, these relationships can be strengthened through carefully crafted formal architecture that both sculpts productive interaction and safeguards against misbehavior. Contracts may also play a vital role in enabling firms to exit collaborative relationships that have run their course in terms of value creation and initiate new, more valuable ones. The capacity to craft contracts, therefore, is a critical capability for any firm seeking to build an ecosystem of effective supplier relationships.

a. Stewart MacCaulay, "Non-Contractual Relations in Business: A Preliminary Study," *American Sociological Review* 55 (1963): 145–164.
b. Sim Sitkin and Nancy L. Roth, "Explaining the Limited Effectiveness of Legalistic 'Remedies' for Trust/Distrust," *Organization Science* 4, no. 3 (1993): 367–392.
c. See Laura Poppo and Todd Zenger, "Do Formal Contracts and Relational Governance Function as Substitutes or Complements?" *Strategic Management Journal* 23, no. 8 (2002): 707–725, and empirical citations in study by Zhi Cao and Fabrice Lumineau, "Revisiting the Interplay between Contractual and Relational Governance," *Journal of Operations Management* 33, (2015): 15–42.
d. Douglass C. North, *Institutions, Institutional Change and Economic Performance* (Cambridge: Cambridge University Press, 1990).

An Unstable Dynamic

Finally, in making decisions around what kind of relationships to have with external suppliers, it is important to realize that the answers to the three questions posed above are unlikely to remain the same over time. There's a tension at the heart of all supplier relationships. Creating valuable relationships demands focus—both in selecting a partner and building collaborative relations with that partner. But an extended focus on a given relationship may generate two potentially negative outcomes. First, the relationship becomes increasingly unique and affords the supplier a growing capacity to extract value from the relationship. Second, as such a relationship deepens, it discourages the firm's departure to what may be a new, more valuable exchange partner.

If you start by using a contest or problem-posting platform to identify external parties that can supply the distinctive knowledge and skills you need to solve problems, you may find that once you've identified those parties, you are motivated to form longer-term alliances or more cooperative relationships with them. Or you may begin with a close collaborative alliance, but discover value in using an auction, RFQ, or contest to elevate bargaining leverage with your existing partner. Switching the terms of the relationship in this way may be inevitable. A study I conducted with Dan Elfenbein examined the e-procurement practices of one of the largest users of online auctions.[14] We observed several intriguing patterns that are key to managing relationships dynamics:

- **Buyers place large value on suppliers with whom they have an historic relationship,** accepting higher bid prices from suppliers with whom they have already done extensive business.

- **Suppliers recognize the value buyers place on relations,** and as they learn what value buyers assign to relations, they attempt to capture more of it.

- **Buyers appear to vacillate over time,** sometimes preferring those with whom they have a previous exchange relationship, and at other times simply preferring suppliers that provide the lowest bid price.

In other words, when a buyer observes suppliers attempting to capture more value through higher prices, it becomes more aggressive in choosing the lowest price. In doing so, it actively cultivates new supply relations. Over time, however, these relationships deepen and the new suppliers elevate prices, seeking to capture some of the value the buyer assigns to the relationships. Once again, the buyer is prompted to look for new lower-priced exchange partners.

The pattern is clear. Relationships are valuable, but your firm must also be on the lookout for new suppliers not only as a source of new competence and lower cost, but also as a vehicle for elevating your bargaining leverage with existing supply relationships. There is no simple, stable equilibrium to be found, but rather an ongoing dynamic in which firms constantly seek to build valuable relationships with optimal external partners, and then position themselves to capture more of the value created.

While effectively crafting market relationships is vital to theory-guided value creation, so too is the organizational design of the activities and assets you choose to keep in-house. Indeed, for the pursuit of many corporate theories, internal design—the structure of incentives, communication and decision rights, and the dynamics by which these are managed—may be the primary vehicles of value creation. Chapter 6 explores these issues.

LESSONS LEARNED

Several important lessons emerge from this discussion:

- **Don't restrict yourself to a single relationship strategy.** There are a host of options from which to choose, ranging from online auctions and crowdsourcing to collaborative alliances and long-term contracts. Each form has virtues and drawbacks, and the saliency of each evolves over time and with context. Close, collaborative partnerships facilitate extensive knowledge sharing and exchange-specific investments. Arm's-length market exchanges, including auctions, simple RFQs, innovation platforms, and contests enable broad access to new exchange partners. You need to learn to tailor your sourcing relations to match the outcomes you seek.

- **In choosing a relationship strategy, ask three questions.** The first question relates to where the knowledge critical to composing the value you envision resides. Do you possess this critical knowledge and therefore require substantial control to shape supplier behavior, or do suppliers already possess the knowledge required? The second question relates to the uniqueness of the product or action you are creating with the supplier. Will it require investment specific to your needs on the part of the supplier or will it benefit more from innovation naturally undertaken by suppliers in a competitive context? The former suggests a collaborative, trust-based relationship; the latter an arm's-length, market-based relationship in which suppliers compete for your business. Finally, can you specify and measure the behavior you want from your supplier? If the answer is yes, then market-based approaches will dominate. If the role of the supplier is not easy to specify, a relationship based strategy may be more appropriate.

- **Be prepared to live with change.** Supplier relations are intrinsically unstable. A study of competitive bidding over time shows that even in a market context, relationships develop as interests align for a while and are then abandoned as the alignment erodes.[15]

And when parties are bound in a close relationship to begin with, there comes a time when a company needs to strengthen its hand by introducing competition in order to prevent the supplier from extracting too much value from the relationship. Strategic leaders optimize value creation by skillfully using contracts to shape supplier relationships dynamically over time, creating possibilities for deepening relationships or closing them down as the company's needs evolve.

PART THREE

Mobilizing for Value

CHAPTER 6

The Dynamic Design of the Organization

O ne of my first teaching experiences was with an evening class of MBA students, at least half of whom
were older than I was and all of whom had a lot more
real-world experience.[1] The evening's topic was organization
design, specifically, the choice to centralize or decentralize—
a choice with profound implications for the structure of
incentives, communication patterns, and decision rights.
We discussed how decentralized designs promote innovation, motivation, and autonomous action, while centralized
designs support control, efficiency, and coordination. My
central (rather predictable) message was about the need to
"design for fit"—to match organizational structure to strategy, an idea that seems on the surface to be very sensible.

After the case discussion ended, a student employed
at McDonnell Douglas (now Boeing) raised his hand and

remarked: "I disagree with everything you have said. I have watched our company move back and forth between central- ization and decentralization repeatedly, and it has nothing to do with what you just described." A classmate chimed in, "I agree completely with [the first student]. Our company has also bounced back and forth between centralization and decentralization. I am quite sure management has no idea what they are doing."

This rather sobering start to my teaching career presented a puzzle that remained with me for years. If fit is the central object of organization design—fit with the environment or fit with strategy—why do firms change their design so often? Are strategies or environments really changing at this pace? Are managers just flailing about to elevate performance?

Perhaps we're asking the wrong question. If you assume that sustained value creation is about having a theory that repeatedly points to new combinations of assets and activi- ties and that these new and evolving combinations require a complex and divergent set of incentives and behaviors, such as both widespread attention to innovation and an obsession with cost reduction, then it quickly becomes apparent that your organization can never in fact fit perfectly to a strat- egy. Quite simply, no internal organizational design (or set of contractual relationships) can configure or target the entire array of complementary behaviors that pursuit of a corpo- rate theory demands. The path to sustained value creation requires pushing the organization in any number of direc- tions. Designing a strategy that attempts to pursue all these directions or accelerates attention to all of these behaviors simultaneously will thus necessarily be less effective than an approach in which designs for pursuing corporate theory are temporally sequenced to emphasize at any point in time a more focused set. Note that in this view, changes in design or emphasis are not driven by dynamics in the environment that call for shifting the target, but rather by the complexity of the target and the limits of design in optimally shaping both individual and organizational attention.

In hindsight, it's ironic that the case I used in that class to illustrate the best-fit theory of organizational structure was Hewlett-Packard. To be sure, it powerfully illustrated the importance of fit—both the consequences of poor fit and the improvement that accompanies correction. But it also turned out to be a case study in the impermanence of organizational design and the need for ongoing, leader-directed dynamics.

There Is No One Best Fit

When I taught that evening's class, HP had completed its first big organizational restructuring. The company had had a long history of extreme decentralization and considerable autonomy. At the beginning of the 1980s, the firm was composed of forty-five small divisions, each crafting, manufacturing, and to a large degree marketing its own specific products. This organizational design had fueled HP's early success as a manufacturer of testing and measurement tools and positioned it as one of the world's most innovative firms.

But by the early 1980s, HP had emerged as a major player in computing, increasingly competing with powerhouse IBM. Unlike its historic businesses in stand-alone test and measurement instruments, whose customers preferred the products dropped on their desks without so much as an instruction manual in a classic geek-to-geek transaction, computing demanded integrated solutions—and the autonomous divisions were now producing incompatible components, supporting redundant development efforts, and creating confused customers. For the first time, HP was confronted with problems and challenges for which its current organizational design provided poor solutions.

To remedy this, beginning in 1983, HP took significant steps toward centralizing manufacturing, marketing, and engineering. The shift quickly worked wonders. The company agreed on common standards and platforms. It eliminated redundancy, developed integrated solutions, and generated happier customers. Financial performance also improved. Moreover, management was convinced that with this new structure, HP had achieved a design that balanced efficiency and coordination with autonomy and innovation. This was where the case ended—a powerful illustration of how design for fit in the wake of a shifting strategy elevates performance.

However, as it turned out, the HP case was just beginning. About the time I was delivering my ill-fated lecture, Hewlett-Packard was actually beginning to reverse its course—decentralizing again. By the late 1980s, innovation at HP had tanked. New products were late. Decision making was mired in administrative processes; even simple decisions were being pushed well up the management ladder. Financial performance had plummeted. In response, HP decentralized its structure, granting divisions considerable autonomy, even moving division heads away from Palo Alto headquarters. Innovation and overall performance improved. With this shift, HP management and securities analysts covering the company were now convinced that HP had achieved proper balance between the need for autonomy's innovation capabilities and centralization's coordination and efficiency.

In 1995, the company again switched course. Its performance had softened and executives perceived a need to coordinate on the development of solutions and integrate their disparate technological expertise. HP once more began a shift toward centralization. As coordination improved, so did performance. The firm's executives and the reports of securities analysts again expressed conviction that HP had achieved a good balance—now a "faster, more competitive company, with an improved product and services offering [and] greater ability to deliver solution."[2]

It should come as no surprise, however, that another structural shift quickly followed, as HP's performance again declined in 1998. Predictably, HP shifted to decentralization, and performance improved for a period. But when HP's first externally appointed CEO, Carly Fiorina, arrived in 1999, she was struck by the inefficiency and lack of coordination across divisions. She immediately centralized HP to a degree unprecedented in its history, and the results were positive.

But sure enough, by 2004, Fiorina faced enormous pressure from both the board and market analysts to decentralize. Most credit her subsequent abrupt dismissal to an unwillingness to listen to the board, particularly an unwillingness to loosen the reins at HP and decentralize. New CEO Mark Hurd, of course, did precisely that, and financial performance accelerated again.

Interestingly, through all of this often wrenching and expensive structural change—this back-and-forth in design—HP had emerged as the world's largest IT firm. Its stock price significantly outperformed all broad market indices over the overall time frame. This strongly suggests that, far from being a bad thing, repeated restructuring may actually be what big companies chasing sustained competitive advantage need to do. Organizational design, in other words, is not a quest for a holy grail of best fit—a stable solution that configures the internal behaviors, investments, decisions, communication, and knowledge flows that will together generate the value you envision. It is fundamentally a dynamic endeavor, even though the strategy and surrounding environment may be stable, even static. HP, for instance, was consistently focused through this whole history on two critical performance dimensions: innovation and efficiency, or what some have labeled exploration and exploitation. When HP decentralized, it was successful in innovation, when it centralized it drove exploitation. Despite its best efforts, and ongoing rhetoric, it was never able to discover a structure that balanced these two permanent concerns. Instead, it achieved success in both by dynamically changing design as the relative importance of the two dimensions changed.

The Complexity Challenge

Even if HP had not been pursuing two somewhat conflicting goals, it would almost certainly still have had to design and redesign as it grew. That's because of another fundamental problem with the assumption that organizational design is stable: there is no way that a single, well-crafted, comprehensive design, anchored on activities that can be measured, can actually generate a highly complex pattern of behaviors all at once. Managers, no matter how skillful, simply cannot engineer the set of incentives and structures and the accompanying social environment that will generate the behaviors, investments, and outcomes that a theory for sustaining repeated value creation (as opposed to the quest for an individual competitive advantage) must imply. Any attempts to craft such a comprehensive, definitive organizational model for competing in a complex world of multiple incentives and behaviors inevitably run into one or more of three problems:

Brain overload

Our brains are just not wired to respond effectively to complex designs that seek to push us in a multitude of directions simultaneously. We are not cognitively programmed to multitask. In fact, one study suggests that those who claim extraordinary multitasking capacity are actually particularly inept.[3] A study published in 2010 by two Paris-based researchers provides an explanation. Participants were assigned first one, then two, and finally three complicated letter-matching tasks, while brain activity was monitored with FMRI technology. When subjects were assigned only one task, both right and left brain hemispheres were focused on performing the singular task. With the introduction of a second task, the left brain focused on one activity, and the right focused on the other, each hemisphere working independently to pursue its respective goal and reward. When a third task was added, participants consistently forgot one of the three tasks. They also made three times as many errors as did those balancing only two tasks. The conclusion was that when we attempt to pursue three goals at the same time, we simply discard one and still perform rather poorly on the remaining two.[4]

It is not surprising, therefore, that organizations struggle when pushed to focus on multiple objectives and performance dimensions. While organizations may divide and conquer by assigning different problems, goals, and objectives to different groups, the approach has clear limits. Many of the problems, goals, and objectives that a corporate theory reveals have application across all groups and individuals and thus, cannot simply be allocated "two per group." Given simple limits to cognitive attention, keeping substantial organizational attention on multiple goals requires sequencing focus and emphasis over time. At a purely cognitive level, asking for concerted attention to an abundance of goals simultaneously is simply wasted effort.[5]

Divided motivations

Even if we set aside individual cognitive limits, a fundamental motivation problem typically plagues efforts to simultaneously direct attention to multiple goals and objectives. The only exception is when the measures and goals revealed by your corporate theory are highly *correlated*—that is, when attention to one goal improves another. Here the behaviors required to generate measure A are substantially the same as those required to generate measure B. Motivating one motivates the other. But this scenario is highly unlikely, and therein lies the challenge. For instance, when the behaviors required to generate autonomous action and innovation differ from the behaviors required to produce efficiency and coordination, how does the employee determine an effective response? Telling employees to maximize current profits, quality, market share, service delivery, future growth in profits, and anything else deemed important leaves them confused about how to prioritize.[6]

When performance metrics differ in accuracy and in the degree to which employees can control them, the challenge in motivation becomes even greater. Activities whose performance dimensions are poorly measured or difficult to control are neglected in favor of those whose metrics produce more measurable results and are more easily controlled. Lack of attention to the tasks with more difficult metrics degrades performance. Steven Kerr's paper, "On the Folly of Reward-ing A While Hoping for B" first captured the essence of this broad problem. Economists later formally designated and further developed this as the *multitasking problem*.[7]

Whatever the label, the implications of the problem are clear. Measuring all dimensions of performance and link-ing rewards to improvement on each does not generate the behavior desired. Attention is selective. Shifting attention to those difficult-to-measure performance dimensions that are often those most central to performance requires dulling incentives for other performance dimensions. For instance, if quantity produced is easily controlled and measured, while quality is difficult to measure and observe, incentives focused on quantity compromise attention to quality. There is simply no combination of incentive composition that gen-erates balanced attention to all critical dimensions. For many firms, the best they can do is essentially provide no incentives at all—a rather poor solution.

Inconsistent choices

Attempts at comprehensive design solutions are further com-plicated by the fact that effective organizational designs are bundles of complementary choices. Design is not an exer-cise in ordering à la carte. Instead, it requires choosing from set menus of design elements that mutually reinforce one another and drive desired behaviors and outcomes. There is thus an inherent discreteness to design. Crafting a design that effectively generates one behavior involves the selection of elements inconsistent with generating another. Attempting to configure an organization that drives all necessary behaviors would involve the selection of highly inconsistent design elements.

Consider, for instance, decentralization and centralization as two distinct designs, each generating a distinct trajectory of behavior. As the HP example that opened this chapter shows, decentralization promotes decision making, communication, and knowledge flows, which fuel exploration and innovation, while decentralization reduces redundancy and facilitates coordination, which fuels efficiency. Each requires differing choices regarding design, incentives, and measurement. Decentralized structures distribute decision rights and performance measures downward and offer powerful incentives. Centralized structures elevate decision rights and performance measure to high levels in the organization and commonly provide lower-level incentives.

Sometimes, of course, corporate theories are strongly aligned with an internally consistent organizational design. Google's corporate theory, for example, calls for a decentralized organizational design. The theory is about the development of cutting-edge, breakthrough technology. Google believes in throwing new technology out into the market to see how it sticks, worrying only afterward about how to exploit it for profit. The emphasis is on hiring the best, brightest, and most creative employees and then providing them with resources to pursue novel opportunities, frequently of their own selection. Google's organization, therefore, is decentralized, granting considerable autonomy to individuals and groups to pursue projects. Incentives tend to mirror those offered in small entrepreneurial firms (that is, they are high-level) and the culture seeks to replicate the same informality and latitude. There are few efforts to integrate the disparate pursuits of these distinct units.

But it's rare that the full set of behaviors and invest-ments foreseen by a corporate theory align so neatly with the outcomes promoted by one of the discrete design options available to managers. As we saw with HP, many firms simul-taneously need the close integration, coordination, and capacity to streamline that centralization delivers, yet also the more autonomous adaptation and innovation that decen-tralization supports. In fact, while the mix may vary, sus-tained value creation for nearly all organizations demands both—the consistent generation of innovative new products and services and consistent improvement in production and distribution efficiency. And, of course, the design problem is even more complex, as there is a considerable array of perfor-mance dimensions that don't align neatly with either central-ization or decentralization.

The Logic of Dynamic Design

How can firms confront these challenges to crafting a com-prehensive design that delivers attention to the multiple goals, objectives, or investments revealed by a corporate the-ory? The key is to view design as a dynamic endeavor rather than static engineering.

For all the rhetoric about the importance of sharing the organization's broader vision, an individual's job at any given moment is likely focused on a rather limited set of organizational goals. There are good reasons for this. As Dan Levinthal and Sendil Ethiraj note, having a focused set of goals and attention provides individuals with the clarity required to motivate action.[8] A single goal or a narrow set of goals matched with the appropriate organizational design motivates focused attention. Such focus accelerates progress, even if that progress is imbalanced relative to the full set performance dimensions or desired behaviors and investments that a corporate theory may reveal. Of course, the patterns of complementarity among performance dimensions and desired behaviors revealed by your theory ensure that extended attention to one elevates the returns to focusing on another in the future.

In other words, if your firm has become extremely lean and efficient in its production and distribution of product, the optimal path to value creation may be generating new innovative products to take advantage of the system. If on the other hand, the organization is tremendously innovative and has generated a pipeline of innovative products, the optimal path to value creation may be to streamline production and distribution. Dynamic design involves selecting the optimal path for the moment on the understanding that you will switch to another in the future.

In this sense, optimal organization design is a bit like sailing into the wind. Attempts to configure main sail, jib, and rudder in order to sail a direct course generate no progress (or negative progress). However, configuring the ship to sail 40 degrees off wind can generate tremendous speed in a useful direction. Yet as the ship travels further in this path, the benefit of a directional shift increases, and the next move is to come about and lay in a new course 40 degrees off wind in the other direction. While each course correction momentarily compromises forward momentum, skillful sailors master these reconfigurations of sail, jib, and rudder to minimize lost time. By periodic tacking, the ship achieves its destination far faster than it could were it to maintain a constant trajectory for an extended period of time.

In much the same way, skilled organizational architects deploy organizational design elements—structure, measures, and incentives—into a coherent form that generates momentum along a valuable trajectory. Moreover, it is precisely the success of the current trajectory, not its failure, that precipitates the benefits of choosing another form and path. The benefits of dynamically shifting design and focus arise in part because the benefits of the current focus do not immediately dissipate upon shifting to another. Thus, an organization's capacity for innovation spurred by decentralization does not immediately disappear with a shift toward centralization and a focus on efficiency. It merely dissipates with inertia. Thus, in pursuing your corporate theory—in attempting to generate this complementary bundle of activities, investments, or behaviors, dynamically choosing the pattern and cadence of change is central. This capacity to dynamically shape attention, focus, and structure is precisely what we observe in effective organizations. The trick is discovering when to do what, *not* how to do it all at once.

Vehicles of Dynamic Design

In managing dynamic design, the leader's first task is to determine the optimal path at any given moment—to constantly monitor the outcomes of the present form and determine at what point switching to another will maximize performance for the firm. Once a decision to change has been taken, there are various ways in which it can be achieved, any and all of which the skilled leader will use. For some firms, dynamic design is best achieved through periodic structural change. For others, however, dynamic design can simply mean a set of sequenced initiatives. Let's briefly consider each.

Structural change

Organizations are massively inert. The communication patterns, work routines, and decision-making processes that comprise organizations resist change. Therefore, to shift the focus and attention of an organization requires more than a gentle nudge. It requires an aggressive shove. Significant structural change provides precisely this shove, as the HP saga illustrates. By switching between centralization and decentralization over twenty-five years, HP shifted its focus between innovation and efficiency over time, arguably generating more of each than it could have achieved were it to have selected best fit at the outset and maintained that structure through the duration. HP's story is not unique. "Dynamic Design at Ford," details Ford's efforts at globalization—a

Dynamic Design at Ford

Two broad performance dimensions are central to global success in automobiles: (1) geographically tailored offerings, responsive to local tastes and preferences and (2) global efficiency (scale economies) in design, procurement, and assembly, frequently achieved by common models, parts, and platforms. These two dimensions are complements in generating performance. Tailored designs increase volume, which provides the scale necessary for efficient manufacturing. Scale provides the efficiency needed to competitively price and sell locally tailored vehicles. However, while local design and global scale are complements to performance, they are substitutes in their production. In other words, organizational designs that drive locally tailored automobile models are inconsistent with organizational designs that generate efficient manufacturing. Attempts to design for both generate weak attention to both. Consequently, Ford found it efficient to shift its structure over the years to pursue one and then the other.

For many decades, the Ford Motor Company was globally decentralized. Each region enjoyed considerable autonomy to design, manufacture, and purchase as it pleased. The result was well-made automobiles tailored to local preferences, but at a very high cost position, given the redundant design and global incompatibility generated by decentralized regional units. To remedy this, in 1994 Ford globally centralized purchasing, engineering, and manufacturing.

Costs declined dramatically as Ford exploited economies of scale, common design platforms, and global purchasing power. Profitability jumped. However, with this centralization, regional managers lost considerable autonomy over product design. Over time, the result was predictable—the cars became poorly adapted to local tastes and circumstances. Soon, there were significant sales declines in international markets: in Europe, the Ford brand dropped from second to fourth place in market share; in Brazil, it lost 4 percentage points in market share.[a] Predictably, in 2000, Ford dramatically decentralized, giving local regional managers autonomy even greater than they had had before 1994.

Thus, decades of divisional autonomy at Ford generated highly innovative and locally responsive designs. But they also yielded poor cross-divisional coordination. Six years of centralization yielded vital coordination, but designs that didn't cater to local preferences. The important point, however, is that Ford's efficiency was unambiguously better off in 2000 for having switched six years previously. It now had common platforms, greater commonality of parts, and perhaps most importantly, reshaped communication patterns and design routines across its global operations. Perhaps Ford should have shifted back sooner or found ways to build platforms that enabled greater local autonomy in design, but it seems hard to dispute that by temporarily centralizing, Ford achieved levels of global efficiency that it could not have achieved had it remained decentralized.

a. Kathleen Kerwin and Keith Naughton, "Remaking Ford," *BusinessWeek,* October 10, 1999.

similar story of vacillating between two distinct structures to achieve both locally tailored designs and global production efficiency.

Of course, patterns of structural change are more complex than simple shifts between centralization and decentralization. Corporate theories reveal multiple dimensions along which organizational design can improve performance. At consulting and accounting firms, for example, success requires leveraging existing relationships, sharing industry-specific knowledge, and transferring best practices. Each one of these activities calls for a distinctive organizational design. A geographic structure facilitates access to relationships held by senior partners. An industry structure facilitates knowledge exchange regarding industry opportunities and trends. A functional or practice structure facilitates best practice sharing by consulting area. Not surprisingly, such firms often cycle through the three. Each structure powerfully pushes on a critical performance dimension. Therefore, for these firms, sustained high performance demands dynamic change, and they discover that sequencing designs generates higher overall performance than sticking with one.

Initiative and goal sequencing

Shifting organizational structure is but one way to redirect focus and effort. Other leaders build and deploy sequences of initiatives that direct attention to different goals, problems, and performance dimensions revealed by a corporate theory.

GE's Jack Welch was a master at sequencing initiatives, each a way to direct attention to a new class of problems or to focus attention on a new performance dimension.

The initiatives cumulatively delivered major changes to GE's focus during Welch's twenty years at the helm. For a while, the focus was on delayering, layoffs, and putting together the right business portfolio through an M&A program, with the aim of positioning the remaining businesses as number one or number two in their industries. GE then became obsessed with Work-Out, a process focused on employee engagement, quick decision making, and solving internal problems and obstacles to performance. Attention then shifted outward, and the organization focused on identifying external best practices and bringing them into the company. GE next turned its attention to services, challenging its business units to increase the portion of their overall sales focused on service from 60 to 80 percent. Finally, Welch trained GE's focus on Six Sigma, with its emphasis on improved quality and reduced cost.

Some firms, often those particularly skillful in acquisitions, are serial sequencers. They have developed scripts—patterns of initiatives that are imposed over time on an acquisition. Danaher, for instance, a firm that has averaged 25 percent compound annual shareholder returns since its inception in 1995, has a "tool box" of dozens of initiatives, processes, and training modules that are deployed as circumstances warrant. These tools and training modules focus on value selling, customer segmentation, product life cycle management, ideation, lean software design, supply chain management, Six Sigma, measurement analysis, and literally dozens of others. They target a range of goals, behaviors, areas of the firm, and performance dimensions. While all of these tools may be deployed at some point in a business's history, there is a common initial sequence that is typically followed post acquisition. Thus, the leader's task in dynamic design is to identify and select the proper sequence of programs, initiatives, or structures.

Whatever form the organizational changes take, major transformations are often accompanied by a change in leadership. Consider 3M, which focused for decades on innovation. Its structure, culture, and policies all targeted new products. Its philosophy was: hire great scientists, provide them with ample resources, and get out of their way. Employees were invited to devote 15 percent of their time to innovative projects that interested them personally. But in the late 1990s, 3M's stock flatlined. There was a general sense that while the company was great at exploring new product terrain, it was not so great at squeezing profits out of the terrain it occupied. For several years, costs had grown at twice the pace of sales.

In response, the board looked for a new CEO who was skilled in execution, and hired an outsider, GE executive Jim McNerny. GE at the time was in its Six Sigma phase, and McNerney brought this passion for it to 3M. For the next four and a half years, McNerney used Six Sigma, coupled with complementary cost cutting and sourcing initiatives, to shift 3M's focus toward exploiting existing product positions by trimming cost and waste. In the process, 3M shifted from being what many described as a playground for scientists to a more centralized and disciplined organization. The result was a sharp spike in profitability and share price.

But in what should be a now-familiar pattern, by the time McNerney moved on to Boeing in 2005, the new emphasis on exploitation and efficiency, while rendering 3M more profitable, had squeezed much of the innovative life out of the company. The board shifted back to an internal CEO steeped in the ways of 3M's success with innovation. Some might conclude that the McNerney years were a misguided departure from leveraging 3M's historic capability, but this interpretation ignores the fact that 3M enters this new phase having solved long-neglected problems and equipped with new routines, new skills, and better operations. However, at this time, the path to improved performance demands an alternative and historically more familiar emphasis. (This story might be instructive for two other firms famed for their historical focus on innovation, but in very different ways; see "A Change for Apple and Google?")

The leadership changes rung in at 3M reflect a common pattern. When a PhD student at Washington University, James Yen, now a professor at Peking University' business school, conducted a fascinating study examining CEO successions at all publicly traded companies from 1992 to 2011. He divided the CEOs into two camps based on their functional background and experience. One group he labeled *output CEOs*; these included those with backgrounds in strategic planning and consulting, entrepreneurship, sales, and R&D. The other group he labeled *throughput CEOs*, who had

A Change for Apple and Google?

One could make a compelling case that Apple would now greatly benefit from a healthy dose of decentralization to cultivate and nurture new ideas and projects. A company so remarkably skillful in design execution might benefit from the breadth of new innovative ideas that decentralization generates. By contrast, Google might benefit from a sustained dose of centralization that would integrate its disparate technologies and applications into more coherent, user-friendly experiences. Admittedly, these revised organizational approaches would certainly have limited functional life spans. Permanently decentralizing the Apple organization would crush its remarkable capacity to develop integrated and effective user experiences. A permanently centralized Google would lose its capacity to broadly innovate.

backgrounds in manufacturing, finance, accounting, process engineering, human resources, and law.

What Yen found is that firms switch between both types of CEO over time. He specifically found that the probability that a firm will switch to a new CEO type conforms to a predictable pattern. The longer a firm has had a CEO of one type, the more likely the next CEO will be of the other. While this simple classification of CEOs into throughput and output hides a wealth of nuance and complexity, the results further support the principle of dynamic design. Firms generate high performance as they pursue complementary goals, behaviors, and investments that corporate theories reveal. However, organizing to pursue all of these at once is infeasible. Throughput and output initiatives are clearly complements to performance. Somewhat ironically, therefore, it may be the success of their initiatives, rather than their failure, that costs CEOs their jobs: their success in doing what they know how to do well triggers the return to doing something different.

This principle is at work not only in the selection of CEOs. Rather, it has application at all levels of the organization. The task in designing organizations is to dynamically construct the value a theory reveals. Theories reveal bundles of goals, behavior, and investments vital to value creation. In order to sequence the organization's focus over time, leadership change may prove a valuable lever.

LESSONS LEARNED

Several key lessons emerge in this chapter:

- **There is no design that will generate all desired behaviors.** Firms need to constantly monitor their current position relative to their corporate theory and the array of behaviors, goals, and investments it reveals. The need for change is frequently and ideally not a symptom of failure, but rather a symptom of success. It is the success of the old design that invites the new—that elevates the benefit of a new approach that invites a new set of complementary investments or accelerates a new set of complementary behaviors.

This logically leads to the second lesson:

- **Organizational design is a problem of dynamic optimization.** The design question is not as simple as, *What is the best organization design for my corporate theory?* Rather, the critical question is, *What is the appropriate organization design now?* Different designs solve different problems; they invite different behaviors and investments. The leader's task is to identify the problem that most needs solving today and design for it, recognizing that tomorrow's problem and the design it needs will be different than today's.

This leads to the third lesson:

- **Timing is everything.** Timing is the most important tool an organizational architect possesses. Like the sailor attempting to sail into the wind, your challenge is to not only put together the necessary change initiatives that will generate real velocity in the direction you select, but to impose them at the correct time. Bad timing dooms what may otherwise be great design.

CHAPTER 7

Leading the
Corporate Theory

I n this book, we have explored the essential paths and
tasks inherent to sustaining corporate growth while creating value. In this final chapter, I turn to the individual's role as a strategic leader and value creator. And let me be
clear: what I write is not intended for only the most senior
managers of large enterprises.

Arguably, the need for and the payoff from sound strategic thinking and strong strategic leadership may be greater
for those leading small, emerging firms than for the CEOs of
large corporations. The strategic genius of most great leaders—
people like Walt Disney, Steve Jobs, or Sam Walton—did not
emerge when they were czars of large corporate empires.
Rather, it emerged while they were guiding fledgling businesses. Early on, they composed powerful corporate theories
that enabled them to build these small entities into empires.

Moreover, strategic leadership is not merely important for those at the helm of corporations. Organizations that sustain value creation are both led by strategic leaders *and* filled with strategic leaders scattered across many areas and all levels of the organization. The capacity to sustain value creation is thus more than a powerful central theory formulated by a CEO perhaps long dead (although admittedly this really helps). They succeed because they are filled with strategic leaders skilled in:

- Assimilating and testing the broader corporate theory

  and

- Developing and pursuing their own local theories of value, sometimes derived from the broader corporate theory, but frequently entirely novel

This novelty, as I have discussed, is essential to value creation. Regardless of position or place in the organization, great strategic leaders see and discover value-creating paths that others cannot. If your vision holds only what others see, you are redundant as a value creator, easily replaced. Your sight offers no unique value.

Not everyone thinks of leadership in terms of value creation. There is a huge body of literature on leadership that focuses on how to powerfully motivate and lead teams. Yet leading and motivating people is but one element on the critical path to value creation. If leadership is leading and motivating, then strategic leading demands the additional skill of deciding *where* to lead. A recent study claimed that this capacity to think and lead strategically was ten times more important to perceptions of effective leadership by peers, subordinates, and senior managers than all other leadership behaviors studied.[1] Yet the idea of strategic thinking as the process of defining where to lead has been relatively ignored—and it merits considerably greater attention.

Strategic leaders consistently identify, evaluate, explore, and ultimately blaze new paths to value creation in whatever corner of the organization they influence. In this sense, strategic leaders are like Vikings, exploring and conquering new lands. As explorers, they have multiple roles. They are mapmakers, developing representations of uncharted territory; navigators, identifying promising paths for exploration; shipbuilders, constantly refining their vessels to increase exploration speed; and skilled sailors, quickly reaching targets through well-sequenced course corrections. To move beyond analogies, however, we could define strategic leaders as performing three key roles as follows:

- Composing powerful, value-creating theories that reveal paths to value creation

- Communicating and selling their theories to key constituents and resource holders

- Dynamically sequencing the attention and focus of those they lead to explore and build the value they envision

A leader who performs all these roles will succeed in motivating and directing others to perform as strategic leaders as well; in a large organization, mobilizing talent in this way enables the leader to shape repeated competitive advantages.

Composing Theories

In the world of entrepreneurship and leadership, much is written about the need for action—for rapid testing of ideas and products at a very early stage. In fact, the central message of the Lean Startup concept—the craze that has captured many managers' imagination these days—is a message about fast action and quick pivots. It describes an approach to innovation built around the "scientific method" in which repeated experimentation continually shifts the trajectory of the enterprise.[2]

Seemingly forgotten in this version of the scientific method is the reality that breakthrough science has far more to do with the theoretical power guiding which experiments will be run than the execution speed of the labs. The message to go out and "do" has vast appeal, as most of us see ourselves as "doers" first, then thinkers. But to fuel significant value creation, additional thinking is needed far more than additional doing.

So what is it that great strategic thinkers think about? They construct theories of value that reveal problems, which if effectively solved will generate enormous value. These problems may be of many types: customer problems (perhaps an unmet need), production problems (perhaps a manufacturing bottleneck), or marketing problems (perhaps an off-target marketing message). Philosopher Karl Popper famously observed that "all life is problem solving."[3] I would perhaps rephrase: all life is problem *finding and solving.* This is certainly true in business.

Strategic leaders are above all great problem finders. They compose theories of value creation that identify novel and "valuable" problems to solve.[4] Albert Einstein is reported to have said: "If I were given one hour to save the planet, I would spend fifty-nine minutes defining the problem and one minute resolving it."[5] Great strategic thinking—thinking that finds and clearly frames a valuable problem dramatically enhances the payoff from problem solving and ensures far more effective doing.

The first task of strategic leaders, therefore, is to assemble a theory that reveals problems that if solved will create value in their domain of influence or control. The bigger the problem revealed, the greater the opportunity for value creation. The best such theories reveal problems that are entirely unknown to others, perhaps unknown to even those who "possess" the problems. The rise of Howard Schultz and Starbucks is a familiar parable in business books. But for me the really interesting point about Howard Schultz is that he uncovered and then pushed a powerful theory of value creation long before he became a reluctant entrepreneur.

While in Milan for a trade show, Schultz visited and enjoyed Italian coffee bars. The experience led him to recognize a valuable problem: US consumers lack access to quality coffee and an attractive physical and social environment in which to consume it. While Schultz was not the first US visitor to appreciate Italian coffee bars, he was perhaps the first to act on a theory that some adaptation of this Italian model might solve a problem that US citizens didn't know they had. When his employers, Starbucks founders, made it clear that they were uninterested in his theory and the central "problems" it revealed, Schultz struck out on his own—only to turn around and buy Starbucks from his former employers.

While the company naturally learned as it pursued experiments, an overall theory of value creation was implicitly in place early on. This theory informed all the experiments, revealing a sequence of subsidiary problems to be solved in product sourcing, store design and format, merchandising mix, store ownership (franchising versus wholly owned), incentives and control, customer education, and vertical integration.

In general, the more complex, novel, and valuable the initial problem identified, the more valuable it is to have a map or theory to guide its exploration. Simple problems require no map—as paths to solutions are rather transparent, and success is about winning the race to the top. On a complex terrain, however, those with a guiding theory of value creation see what others can't, including paths to complete and valuable solutions. It was Steve Jobs's unique theory about what consumers would value that revealed entirely new problems and previously unseen paths to solutions. The result was a completely novel trajectory of experiments. The difference between strategic successes and failures has far more to do with the quality of the theory that's behind a company's experiments than with the pace and number of the experiments. Sustaining value creation, by extension, requires better theories—not faster-paced pivots.

Selling the Theory

Unfortunately, the inherent novelty of valuable strategic thinking means that leaders need to persuade others to pursue the paths to value creation that they identify. Just as senior managers face a clear challenge in selling investors on their corporate theories—precisely those theories that hold the promise of delivering the greatest value—less senior strategic leaders face a parallel challenge. The most valuable strategic thinking both personally (in advancing a career) and organizationally (in advancing value creation) is novel, and novelty almost always confronts resistance. Ben Horowitz, cofounder of the venture capital firm Andreesen Horowitz, observes that those who build great companies are always "ridiculed along the way," but argues: "If you are driven by social signals, you shouldn't be an entrepreneur."[6] This is a valuable piece of wisdom for all strategic leaders, not merely entrepreneurs. For better or worse, strategic leaders must be thoroughly convinced themselves before trying to persuade others.

And the difficulty of selling a theory or persuading others of the validity of your strategic thought escalates exponentially with its novelty. Although Howard Schultz was a wildly successful entrepreneur, as an employee, he failed as a strategic leader in his attempts to persuade his superiors of the value of his thinking. It's a familiar story, and often the failure to convince a current employer precipitates entre-preneurship. Although this is not necessarily a bad outcome for the new entrepreneur, it is a missed opportunity for the company—all the more so as the original theory behind the forced entrepreneurship very likely involved exploiting assets and capabilities the company already had. The strate-gic leader able to persuade an existing employer, therefore, is arguably more likely to succeed in making a theory real than a strategic leader forced to start more or less from scratch. And it's not just the bosses that need convincing. Everyone the leader must work with—both inside and outside the corporation—will have to be sold on the idea.

After composing a theory of value creation, therefore, a key task is to craft compelling language that enables oth-ers to see what you see—clarity of expression and clear logic are critical to enrolling others. Research in psychology also highlights this point. For example, in cases in which minority groups have persuaded a hitherto indifferent majority, con-fidently and consistently articulated positions presented with the perception of being unbiased have more often suc-ceeded than attempts to persuade through other ways and means.[7] So although much has been written about the impor-tance of garnering power and skillful politicking as vehicles for imposing your will and vision in an organization, more important is a powerful and valid conception of a path to value that you can persuasively articulate. Steve Jobs was no politician, as biographies attest, but he was masterful with language—language that he used to powerfully articulate his theories of value creation. A vivid metaphor can powerfully convey a unique idea or perspective, or a theory. In leading the team that generated the first complete product manifestation of his theory, the Macintosh, Jobs sometimes characterized the object of design as a Porsche, at others as a machine that looked "friendly." This language painted a valuable image and provided general principles to guide the pattern of experiments that would ultimately result in this remarkable product.

The task of strategic leaders is to persuade others to pursue their novel path to value creation. Edicts are ineffective. As Larry Bossidy, former CEO of Allied Signal, put it: "The day when you could yell and scream and beat people into good performance is over. Today you have to appeal to them by helping them see how they can get from here to there, by establishing some credibility, and by giving them some reason to help to get there. Do all those things, and they'll knock down doors."[8] If as discussed in this book, corporate theories should drive a wide-ranging set of decisions, involving the composition, investments, and structure of the corporation, it is critical that strategic leaders enable others to see what they see and be convinced of the vision's merits.

Navigating Organizational Dynamics

As this book has made clear, powerful theories of value creation reveal myriad problems to solve, actions to pursue, and experiments to undertake. At the same time, serious cognitive, behavioral, and organizational constraints limit an firm's capacity to attend to all paths to value creation simultaneously. Strategic leaders recognize that focusing attention on particular performance metrics and problems is far more effective in creating that value than drawing attention and focus to the vast array all at once. Strategic leadership is about prioritizing. It is about selecting the optimal current path, at any given time, to value creation.

A strategic leader, therefore, must be skillful in navigating the dynamics of organizational focus and attention. This involves having not only a clear sense of what the organization must do, but an even clearer of sense of timing—a sense of who to persuade to do what, when, and where. Strategic leaders steer an organization's focus, using organizational levers and communication platforms to direct the exploratory, value-creating efforts of others. Recall Jack Welch's two decades at the helm of GE. His successful leadership was a product of both his strategic vision and his remarkable knack for constantly shifting the focus and attention of the organization to explore new paths of value creation, pushing GE managers to constantly tackle new sets of problems. For a while, the focus was the competitive position and scale of business units, then it shifted to empowering employees to solve more local problems, then to global outreach, then to expanding service offerings, and then to a focus on quality and process improvement. Interspersed among these were a wide range of other initiatives. By shifting focus, Welch shifted the domain of the firm's problem-finding and problem-solving efforts. The result was a remarkable path of value creation. In a similar vein, Michael Eisner's brilliance during his first decade at Disney was his capacity to consistently push the organization to discover a succession of new value-creating investments consistent with the Disney theory.

One of the most powerful tools in shaping a company's focus and attention is organizational design. Different designs are likely to encourage different approaches to problem finding and problem solving. For instance, as discussed in chapter 6, more centralized designs may focus attention on problems that promote efficiency and coordination, while more decentralized designs may fuel innovation. But organizational design is a difficult art, requiring the skillful management of trade-offs and paradoxes. There is no one design that will drive all of the desired value-generating behaviors. Moreover, once a company adopts a structure that highlights one set of problems, it often finds over time that the benefits from changing the structure and focus become increasingly large. It is up to the strategic leader to figure out the proper timing and scope of organizational change.

Many CEOs are one-trick ponies, able to push at most a single button with success. When that trajectory runs out of gas, or when the optimal path of value creation shifts, they are incapable of providing the requisite new focus or direction. Their tenure is generally short. Long-lived CEOs have both a broad vision and a capacity to dynamically navigate toward it, recognizing the limitation of any one path in realizing the full value their theory envisions. Strategic leaders throughout the organization are no different. They recognize their inability to pursue all at once the vast array of dimensions requisite for sustaining value creation. Instead, they lead by choosing today's trajectory.

This book began with a description of the difficulty that organizations face in sustaining value creation. The need to relentlessly create value while exceeding investors' expectations sets an enormously high bar. Regardless of your role, whether CEO or aspiring manager, your efforts alone will inevitably prove insufficient.

Stripped to its essentials, therefore, the challenge of strategic leadership is twofold: you have to have a big idea, then you must be able to inspire and motivate others to think strategically about how to realize that big idea. The more complex and unique the idea, the more valuable it is, but also the more you will need more than just your own brilliant strategic thinking or skilled problem finding and problem solving. To pursue a big idea, you will need to engage others in problem finding and problem solving alongside you. You need others engaged in strategic thinking and skillfully persuading others to engage. Succeed in this—thanks to a sound theory, well-articulated, and supported by your organizational decisions—and you will create a powerful virtuous dynamic: as people improve in confidence and clarity of expression, their own ability to persuade and motivate others increases.

The great German conductor Herbert von Karajan was a keen horseman, and he often liked to compare his profession with his sport. Conducting an orchestra, he once claimed, was like leading a horse over a hurdle: "You cannot jump the fence for them. You have to point them in the right direction."[9] The challenge, in other words, is getting the horse to jump the fence or the orchestra to play the music *in just the right way.* To do that, you need a personal vision about what the right way basically is—what needs to be done for a piece of music to sound "right." You have to be able to explain your vision to the musicians in the orchestra, and you have to manage the rehearsals in ways that encourage the musicians to produce the sounds you seek.

As a strategic leader seeking to move your organization beyond competitive advantage—on to a trajectory of sustained value creation, your tasks are to be skilled composers and conductors, seeing value others cannot and then constantly orchestrating the composition of activities and assets across time, with proper tempo and dynamics. Succeed here, and investor applause will be resounding.

NOTES

Introduction

1. Charles S. Pierce, "The Logic of Abduction," *Pierce's Essays in the Philosophy of Science* ed. Vincent Tomas (New York: Liberal Arts Press, 1957), 195–205.

2. Michael Porter, "What Is Strategy?" *Harvard Business Review*, November–December 1996.

3. Dan Lovallo and Lenny T. Mendonca, "Strategy's Strategist: An Interview with Richard Rumelt," *McKinsey Quarterly*, August 2007.

4. Ibid.

5. Thomas J. Peters and Robert H. Waterman, Jr., *In Search of Excellence: Lessons from America's Best-Run Companies* (New York: Harper & Row, 1982).

6. John A. Byrne, "Oops! Who's Excellent Now?" *BusinessWeek*, November 5, 1984.

7. James C. Collins and Jerry I. Porras, *Built to Last: Successful Habits of Visionary Companies* (New York: HarperBusiness, 1994).

8. James C. Collins, *Good to Great: Why Some Companies Make the Leap—and Others Don't* (New York: HarperBusiness, 2001).

9. Bing Cao, Bin Jiang, and Tim Koller, "Sustaining Top-Line Growth," *McKinsey Quarterly*, May 2011.

Chapter 1

1. This chapter has greatly benefited from collaboration with Teppo Felin, most particularly in Teppo Felin and Todd R. Zenger, "Entrepreneurs as Theorists: On the Origins of Collective Beliefs and Novel Strategies," *Strategic Entrepreneurship Journal* 3, no. 2 (2009): 127–146; and Teppo Felin and Todd R. Zenger, "Strategy, Problems, and a Theory for the Firm," *Organization Science* 27, no. 1 (2016): 222–231.

The chapter has also benefited from collaboration with Nick Argyres (see Nick Argyres and Todd R. Zenger, "Capabilities, Transactions Costs, and Firm Boundaries," *Organization Science* 23 (2012): 1643–1657).

2. In James Burke, PBS Documentary *Connections,* 1979.

3. In Josh Ong, "Steve Jobs' 'Lost Interview:' Design is keeping 5,000 things in your brain," appleinsider, November 15, 2011.

4. In "The Theory of the Business" (*Harvard Business Review*, September–October 1994), Peter Drucker also suggests that firms have a "theory of the business," sometimes correct and sometimes incorrect, that guides their choices.

Over the past two decades, psychologists have developed a new and increasingly influential theory of how we learn. The approach, oddly titled the *theory theory,* suggests that from infancy, we learn by composing and acting on theories of our surrounding world. For instance, infants acquire language by composing a theory of language and grammar, which they then use in a predictive manner to compose sentences that often bear little resemblance to any they have ever heard (Noam Chomsky, *The Logical Structure of Linguistic Theory* [New York: Plenum, 1975]). Thus we learn to navigate our complex world by acting much like scientists—cognitively composing theories, formulating hypotheses, and running experiments. Our theories serve to guide actions, providing unique vision and serving as filters through which we interpret our observations and update our actions. By logical extension, individuals who achieve high levels of cognitive development are enormously adept at crafting accurate theories, generating hypotheses, processing feedback, and then appropriately updating these theories.

5. The logic surrounding "insight" draws from the resource-based perspective in the strategy literature (see Jay Barney, "Firm Resources and Competitive Advantage," *Journal of Management* 17, no. 1 [1991]: 99–120; Richard P. Rumelt, "Towards a Strategic Theory of the Firm," in *Competitive Strategic Management*, ed. Robert B. Lamb [Englewood Cliffs, NJ: Prentice-Hall, 1984] 556–570).

6. Recorded in John Steele Gordon, *The Business of America* (New York: Walker & Company, 2001). On his version of the automobile, Henry Ford commented: "I invented nothing new. I simply assembled into a car the discoveries of other men behind which were centuries of work."

7. A consensus has arguably emerged in the strategy literature that is consistent with Rumelt's statement that "a firm's competitive position is defined by a bundle of unique resources and relationships" (Richard P. Rumelt, "Towards a Strategic Theory of the Firm," in *Competitive Strategic Management,* ed. Robert B. Lamb [Englewood Cliffs, NJ: Prentice-Hall, 1984], 556–570). Firms are thought to acquire positions of advantage by assembling or "organizing" sets of unique and complementary resources, activities, or assets that together form unique firm capabilities. These advantageous positions emerge through relationships among resources (or activities and assets) that are superadditive or complementary, such that combining the resources in a bundle creates more value than the sum of the values of the resources if left unbundled (for example, see Raphael Amit and Paul J. H. Shoemaker, "Specialized Assets and Organizational Rent," *Strategic Management Journal* 14 (1993): 33–47; and Cynthia Montgomery and Birger Wernerfelt, "Diversification, Ricardian Rents and Tobin's q," *Rand Journal of Economics* 19 (1988): 623–633). Other scholars use terms such as "interconnectedness of asset stocks" (Ingemar Dierickx and Karel Cool, "Asset Stock Accumulation and Sustainability of Competitive Advantage," *Management Science* 35, no. 12 (1989): 1504–1513) and "integrated set[s] of choices about activities" (Pankaj Ghemawat, *Strategy and the Business Landscape,* 2nd edition [Englewood Cliffs, NJ: Prentice Hall, 2005]) to describe the origins of these capabilities and their resulting rents.

8. Walter Isaacson, *Steve Jobs* (New York: Simon & Shuster, 2011), 85.

9. Ibid, 561.

10. Xerox did, of course, try to commercialize this technology itself. They introduced their own computer three years before the Macintosh, priced at $16K, targeting the word processing market. It was clunky and unsuccessful.

11. "A Brief History: Origins," AT&T, http://www.corp.att.com/history/history1.html, accessed January 27, 2016.

12. Michael A. Noll, "The Bell Breakup @ 15 Years," *tele.com* 4, no. 13 (June 21, 1999), http://www.lexisnexis.com.libproxy.wustl.edu/us/lnacademic/auth/checkbrowser.do?rand=0.39216079013306393&cookieState=0&ipcounter=1&bhcp=1.

13. The Telecommunications Act did permit AT&T to provide local service again.

14. Michael G. Rukstad, Tyrrell Levine, and Carl Johnston, "Breakup of AT&T: Project 'Grand Slam'" case study 701127 (Boston: Harvard Business School, 2001), 5.

15. Ibid, 11.

16. Ibid.

17. Kurt Lewin, *Field Theory in Social Science: Selected Theoretical Papers by Kurt Lewin* (London: Tavistock, 1952), 169.

Chapter 2

1. Gary S. Becker, *The Economic Approach to Human Behavior* (Chicago: University of Chicago Press, 1976).

2. For discussion of empirical results on the returns to acquisitions see Jens Kengelbach and Alexander Roos, *Riding the Next Wave in M&A: Where are the Opportunities to Create Value?* BCG Report (2011); Michael Bradley, Anand Desai, and E. Han Kim, "Synergistic Gains from Corporate Acquisitions and Their Division Between the Stockholders of Target and Acquiring Firms," *Journal of Financial Economics* 21, no. 1 (1988): 3–40; Todd Hazelkorn, Marc Zenner, and Anil Shivdasani, "Creating Value with Mergers and Acquisitions," *Journal of Applied Corporate Finance* 16, no. 2–3 (2004): 81–90.

3. The winner's curse is sometimes referred to as a *Pyrrhic victory*. In 280 BC, King Pyrrhus of Epirus defeated the Romans at Heraclea and then at Asculum in 279 BC, but in the process suffered tremendous casualties. These victories prompted the king to comment: "Another such victory and I come back to Epirus alone."

4. Michael Bradley, Anand Desai, and E. Han Kim, "Synergistic Gains from Corporate Acquisitions and Their Division Between the Stockholders of Target and Acquiring Firms," *Journal of Financial Economics* 21, no. 1 (1988): 3–40.

5. See Mark L. Sirower and Sumit Sahni, "Avoiding the 'Synergy Trap': Practical Guidance on M&A Decisions for CEOs and Boards," *Journal of Applied Corporate Finance* 18, no. 3 (Summer 2006): 83–95.

6. Todd Hazelkorn, Marc Zenner, and Anil Shivdasani, "Creating Value with Mergers and Acquisitions," *Journal of Applied Corporate Finance* 16, no. 2–3 (2004): 81–90.

7. Sirower and Sahni, "Avoiding the 'Synergy Trap.'"

8. Hazelkorn, Zenner, and Shivdasani, "Creating Value with Mergers and Acquisitions."

9. Lubomir P. Litov and Todd Zenger, "Do Investors Value Uniqueness in Markets for Strategy? Evidence from Mergers and Acquisitions," University of Utah working paper (2014).

Chapter 3

1. The ideas expressed in this chapter have benefitted from collaborations with Lubomir Litov, Mary Benner, and Patrick Moreton. See Lubomir Litov, Patrick Moreton, and Todd Zenger, "Corporate Strategy, Analyst Coverage, and the Uniqueness Discount," *Management Science* 58, no. 10 (2012): 1797–1815; Mary Benner and Todd Zenger, "The Lemons Problem in Markets for Strategy," *Strategy Science*, forthcoming.

2. David Lieberman and Matt Krantz, "Is Kraft's 19B takeover of Cadbury a Sweet Deal? Warren Buffet has Doubts," *USA Today*, January 20, 2010.

3. See "Kraft Split to Unlock Value but Stock Stuck for Now," *Forbes*, December 9, 2011.

4. See Friedrich A. Hayek, "The Use of Knowledge in Society," *American Economic Review* 35 (1945): 519–530.

5. James Surowiecki's best-selling *The Wisdom of Crowds* (New York: Doubleday, 2004) makes a compelling case for the superiority of crowds in guiding behavior.

6. Michael C. Jensen and William Meckling, "Theory of the Firm: Managerial Behavior, Agency Costs and Ownership Structure," *Journal of Financial Economics* 3, no. 4 (1976): 305–360.

7. Akerlof shared this award with Michael Spence and Joseph Stiglitz, who also substantially contributed to the early development of information economics.

8. George Akerlof, "The Market for Lemons: Quality Uncertainty and the Market Mechanism," *Quarterly Journal of Economics* 84 (1970): 488–500.

9. Brett Trueman, M. H. Franco Wong, and Xiao-Jun Zhang, "The Eyeballs Have It: Searching for the Value in Internet Stocks," in "Studies on Accounting Information and the Economics of the Firm," supplement, *Journal of Accounting Research* 38 (2000): 137–162.

Notes

10. Jeffrey Chaffkin, PaineWebber Research Note on Monsanto Corporation, November 2, 1999.

11. Harrison Hong, Terence Lim, and Jeremy C. Stein, J. "Bad News Travels Slowly: Size, Analyst Coverage, and the Profitability of Momentum Strategies," *Journal of Finance* 55, no. 1 (2000): 265–295; Pieter T. Elgers, May H. Lo, and Ray J. Pfeiffer, "Delayed Security Price Adjustments to Financial Analysts' Forecasts of Annual Earnings," *Accounting Review* 76, no. 4 (2001): 613–623.

12. Richard M. Frankel, S. P. Kothari, and Joseph Weber, "Determinants of the Informativeness of Analyst Research," MIT Sloan Working Paper No. 4243-02, (2003), http://dx.doi.org/10.2139/ssrn.304483; Thomas Lys and Sunkyu Sohn, "The Association Between Revisions of Financial Analysts' Earnings Forecasts and Security-Price Changes," *Journal of Accounting and Economics* 13, no. 4 (1990): 341–363. As Jensen and Meckling argue: "The benefits of the security analysis activity [are] reflected in the higher capitalized value of the ownership claims to corporations . . . " ("Theory of the Firm").

13. Lubomir Litov, Patrick Moreton, and Todd Zenger, "Corporate Strategy, Analyst Coverage, and the Uniqueness Discount," *Management Science* 58, no. 10 (2012): 1797–1815.

14. Ezra W. Zuckerman, "Focusing the Corporate Product: Securities Analysts and De-Diversification," *Administrative Science Quarterly* 45, no. 3 (2000): 591–619.

15. Ravi Bhushan, "Firm Characteristics and Analyst Following," *Journal of Accounting and Economics* 11, nos. 2–3 (1989): 255–274. Yet another study found that when managers unbundle their conglomerates through spin-offs and carve-outs in response to capital market pressure, the aggregate level of analyst coverage increases, as does the accuracy of analysis (i.e., the capacity to accurately predict future performance); see Stuart C. Gilson, Paul M. Healy, Christopher F. Noe, and Krishna G. Palepu, "Analyst Specialization and Conglomerate Stock Breakups," *Journal of Accounting Research* 39 (December 2001): 565–582.

16. Litov, Moreton, and Zenger, "Corporate Strategy, Analyst Coverage, and the Uniqueness Discount."

17. Gilson et al., "Analyst Specialization and Conglomerate Stock Breakups."

18. Ezra W. Zuckerman, "Focusing the Corporate Product: Securities Analysts and De-Diversification," *Administrative Science Quarterly* 45, no. 3 (2000): 591–619.

19. For a discussion of the usefulness of this type of analyst coverage see Bruce K. Billings, William L. Buslepp, and G. Ryan Huston, "Worth the Hype? The Relevance of Paid-for Analyst Research for the Buy-and-Hold Investor," *The Accounting Review* 89 (2014): 903–931.

20. Dan Roberts, "Georgia Pacific decides to leave the spotlight," *The Financial Times*, November 15, 2005, 29.

21. Admittedly, there is growing research in finance examining the temporal horizon of executive pay. However, in practice, CEO rewards remain quite focused on increasing the present or short-term value of the enterprise as reflected in capital markets.

Chapter 4

1. The ideas in this chapter have particularly benefitted from collaborations with Nick Argyres, Jackson Nickerson, Teppo Felin, and Lyda Bigelow.

2. See Otto Friedrich, *Decline and Fall: The Struggle for Power at a Great American Magazine* (New York: Harper and Row, 1970).

3. See Friedrich A. Hayek, "The Use of Knowledge in Society," *American Economic Review* 35 (1945): 519–530.

4. See Oliver Williamson, *The Economic Institutions of Capitalism* (New York: Simon and Schuster, 1985); Benjamin Klein, Robert Crawford, and Armen Alchian, "Vertical Integration, Appropriable Quasi-Rents, and the Competitive Contracting Process," *Journal of Law and Economics* 21, no. 2 (1978): 297–326.

5. D. H. Robertson, quoted in Ronald Coase, "The Nature of the Firm," *Economica* 4, no. 16 (1937): 386–405.

6. This is a paraphrase of MIT's Robert Gibbons statement: "the cost of control is the loss of initiative." See Robert Gibbons, "Four (Formalizable) Theories of the Firm, *Journal of Economic Behavior and Organization,* 58 (2005): 206.

7. For a discussion of this argument and supporting research see Jack A. Nickerson and Todd R. Zenger, "Envy, Comparison Costs, and

the Economic Theory of the Firm," *Strategic Management Journal* 29, no. 13 (2008): 1429–1449.

8. See Paul Milgrom and John Roberts, "An Economic Approach to Influence Activities in Organizations," *American Journal of Sociology* 94 Supplement (1988): S154–S179.

9. "John Harvard's Journal: 'Extraordinary Bonuses,'" *Harvard Magazine* 106, no. 4 (2004): 69–73.

Chapter 5

1. Friedrich Hayek, "The Use of Knowledge in Society," *American Economic Review* 35, no. 4 (1945): 519–530.

2. In 1987, Japan's MITI commented the simple declaration that "Japanese manufacturing owes its competitive advantage and strength to its subcontracting structure." Quoted in Jeffrey H. Dyer and William G. Ouchi, "Japanese-Style Partnerships: Giving Companies a Competitive Edge," *MIT Sloan Management Review* 35 (Fall 1993).

3. For a more complete discussion see Dyer and Ouchi, "Japanese-Style Partnerships."

4. Michael A. Cusumano and Akira Takeishi, "Supplier Relations and Management: A Survey of Japanese, Japanese-Transplant, and U.S. Auto Plants," *Strategic Management Journal* 12, no. 8 (1991): 563–588.

5. EIU Global Executive Survey, Anderson Consulting.

6. Michael Gerlach, *Alliance Capitalism: The Social Organization of Japanese Business* (Berkeley: University of California Press, 1992); Jeffrey H. Dyer and Harbir Singh, "The Relational View: Cooperative Strategy and Sources of Interorganizational Competitive Advantage," *Academy of Management Review* 23, no. 4 (1998): 660–679.

7. See Internet World Stats: Usage and Population Statistics, www.internetworldstats.com.

8. Mark Doms, "The Boom and Bust in Information Technology Investment," *FRBSF Economic Review* (2004): 19–34.

9. For instance, in a study I jointly conducted with Dan Elfenbein examining one of the largest users of these reverse procurement auctions, the lowest bidder was selected only about half of the time.

10. An AT Kearney consulting report claimed that while standard procurement methods enabled buyers to interact with about 25 percent of key suppliers in a field, e-procurement provided access to 98 percent. See Olivia Korostelina, "Online Reverse Auctions: A Cost-Saving Inspiration for Businesses," *Dartmouth Business Journal* (March 2012).

11. MIT's Eric von Hippel has been the most vocal proponent of this position.

12. Kevin J. Boudreau Karim R. Lakhani, "Using the Crowd as an Innovation Partner," *Harvard Business Review*, April 2013.

13. Hayek, "The Use of Knowledge in Society."

14. See Daniel Elfenbein and Todd Zenger, "Creating and Capturing Value in Repeated Exchange Relationships: Managing a Second Paradox of Embeddedness," Olin Business School Working Paper, 2016.

15. Ibid.

Chapter 6

1. The ideas in this chapter have particularly benefitted from a long standing academic collaboration with Jackson Nickerson at Washington University in St. Louis. See Jack A. Nickerson and Todd R. Zenger "Being Efficiently Fickle: A Dynamic Theory of Organizational Choice." *Organization Science* 13 (2002): 547–566; and Peter Boumgarden, Jack A. Nickerson, and Todd R. Zenger, "Ambidexterity, Vacillation, and Organizational Performance," *Strategic Management Journal* 33 (2012): 587–610.

2. Hewlett-Packard. 1998. Annual Report. Thompson Research. Available at: http://research.thomsonib.com/.

3. Eyal Ophir, Clifford Nass, and Anthony D. Wagner, "Cognitive Control in Media Multitaskers," *Proceedings of the National Academy of Sciences of the United States of America* 106, no. 37 (2009): 15583–15587.

4. Sylvain Charron and Etienne Koechlin, "Divided Representation of Concurrent Goals in the Human Frontal Lobes," *Science* 328, no. 360 (2010): 360–363.

5. Interestingly, in Hoshin Kanri, the Japanese predecessor to Balanced Scorecard, high-level initiatives are restricted to one or two at any

given time (cited in Sendil K. Ethiraj and Daniel A. Levinthal, "Hoping for A to Z While Rewarding Only A: Complex Organizations and Multiple Goals," *Organization Science* 20, no. 1 (2009): 4–21.

6. Michael Jensen more precisely remarked that it is "logically impossible to maximize in more than one dimension at the same time unless dimensions are what are known as monotonic transformations of one another" (Michael C. Jensen, *Foundations of Organizational Strategy* [Cambridge, MA: Harvard University Press, 2001]).

7. And then formally modeled as a multitasking problem by economists Bengt Holmstrom and Paul Milgrom. See Bengt Holmstrom and Paul Milgrom, "Multi-task Principal-Agent Analyses: Incentive Contracts, Asset Ownership, and Job Design," *Journal of Law, Economics, and Organization* 7 Special Issue (1991): 24–52.

8. Ethiraj and Levinthal, "Hoping for A to Z."

Chapter 7

1. Robert Kabocoff, "Develop Strategic Thinkers Throughout Your Organization," *Harvard Business Review*, February 7, 2014, https://hbr.org/2014/02/develop-strategic-thinkers-throughout-your-organization.

2. Eric Ries, *The Lean Startup: How Today's Entrepreneurs Use Continuous Innovation to Create Radically Successful Businesses* (New York: Crown Publishing Group, 2011).

3. Popper made this comment in a 1991 lecture, and this also became the title of a posthumously published compilation of his essays. See Karl Popper, *All Life is Problem Solving* (New York: Routlege, 1999).

4. Interestingly, the Nobel Prize–winning economist Herbert Simon describes strategies as "problem representations." See Herbert Simon, "Bounded Rationality and Organizational Learning," *Organization Science* 2, no. 1 (1991): 125–134.

5. Quoted in Dwayne Spradlin, "Are You Solving the Right Problem?" *Harvard Business Review*, September 2012, https://hbr.org/2012/09/are-you-solving-the-right-problem.

6. Ben Horowitz in an interview on the Product Hunt. This quote and others can be found at "Ben Horowitz's Best Startup Advice," Product Hunt, September 10, 2015, https://www.producthunt.com/live/ben-horowitz.

7. For a discussion see Serge Moscovici, *Social Influence and Social Change* (London: Academic Press, 1976); and Serge Moscovici, "Toward a Theory of Conversion Behavior," *Advances in experimental social psychology* (ed. L. Berkowitz) 13 (1980): 209–239.

8. Jay Conger, "The Necessary Art of Persuasion," *Harvard Business Review*, May–June 1988.

9. Quoted in Peter Quantrill, "Hammer of the Gods," *Gramophone*, January 2008.

INDEX

Note: page numbers followed by *f* refer to figures.

ACKNOWLEDGMENTS

It was perhaps fifteen years ago that my father first posed the question, "When are you going to write a book?" Of course, this was code for, "When are you going to write something for an audience other than academics—for real people?" What followed was my lecture on the trickle-down flow of knowledge from academics to "real people," followed by an active discussion on the pace of that trickle. I suspect, however, that without my father's prod, the ideas in this book would still remain scattered across academic manuscripts. In more recent years, his question simply turned to, "How's the book?" Both of my parents instilled in me a desire to ask and pursue important and interesting questions, for which I am tremendously grateful.

Parsing out the origin of ideas is an impossible task, especially given the bias toward hubris that afflicts us all. I am enormously indebted to coauthors and colleagues who have profoundly shaped and contributed to the ideas in this book. I am confident the debt is larger than I even recognize. Valuable creations are always clever recombinations of others' ideas, and this effort is no different.

I spent the first twenty-four years of my academic career teaching at Washington University's Olin Business School. It was there that most of the ideas in this book took root.

Acknowledgments

I am grateful for Washington University's support and its willingness to gamble on a young, inexperienced PhD graduate many years ago. It was an enormously rewarding experience to help assemble a remarkable group of colleagues there and to enjoy the intellectual rewards of what has become one of the country's top strategy groups. I am also grateful to the David Eccles School of Business at the University of Utah, where I have spent the past two years. Here, too, I have been blessed with remarkable colleagues who challenge my thinking and ideas.

I am particularly grateful for my academic collaborations with Jackson Nickerson, Teppo Felin, Nick Argyres, Dan Elfenbein, Bill Hesterly, Patrick Moreton, Lubo Litov, Mary Benner, and Laura Poppo. These collaborations have importantly shaped chapters within the book. I am also grateful for extensive conversations and collaborations with other colleagues, including Jay Barney, Bart Hamilton, Anne Marie Knott, Lyda Bigelow, Lamar Pierce, Gary Miller, Tomasz Obloj, Nicolai Foss, Peter Klein, Rob Wuebker, Russ Coff, Adina Sterling, and Zeke Hernandez. I am also grateful for conversations, support, or collaborations with former PhD students, Sergio Lazzarini, Chihmao Hsieh, Jeffrey Huang, Carl Vieregger, James Yen, Tim Gubler, and Ryan Cooper, as well as initial research assistance from Chris Brennan. I am further grateful for hundreds of executive MBA and MBA students at both Washington University and University of Utah with whom I have tested the content of the book and have burdened with draft chapters as a course text. Their comments and reactions, positive or negative, have profoundly shaped the evolution of this work.

Acknowledgments

My ideas were also shaped by remarkable years spent at UCLA as a PhD student in strategy in the mid-1980s. Three important theoretical events in the strategy field transpired during those years. First was the emergence of the concept of competitive advantage and industrial organization economics as a central framework in teaching strategy. Second was the emergence of organizational economics as an increasingly dominant strategic logic in thinking about strategy and organization. Third was the development of the resource-based perspective. During my years as a PhD student, UCLA played a central role in fueling the latter two theoretical trends. All three are pivotal to the intellectual foundations of this book. I am grateful for classes or conversations with UCLA faculty at the time: William Ouchi, Jay Barney, Richard Rumelt, Ben Klein, Harold Demsetz, Eric Rasmusen, and Barbara Lawrence.

Harvard Business Review Press's editorial director Tim Sullivan, my editor David Champion, and my literary agent Giles Anderson have each played a pivotal role in the emergence and publication of this manuscript. Tim saw initial promise in a far too academic proposal with initial chapters that I thought spoke to real people but needed considerable work to actually do so. He has championed the ideas in this book through the review process, both at Harvard Business Review Press and at *Harvard Business Review*. David worked with me to develop two *HBR* articles from the initial draft chapters: "What Is the Theory of Your Firm?" (November 2013) and "Strategy: The Uniqueness Challenge" (June 2014). David has been a remarkable editor in developing the book

205

manuscript, helping me with the transition from writing for an academic audience to writing for a general audience. He has challenged me to simplify what I say and, in the process, clarify and refine the underlying logic. I have tried to be a good student. Meanwhile, Giles was instrumental in helping me polish and then successfully re-pitch the book proposal to Harvard Business Review Press.

Above all, I am grateful for my wife, Shawn, who has been exceptionally supportive throughout my academic career. After hearing about this phantom book for so many years, she too took up the cadence of "how's the book?" She has been a remarkable companion and partner in our most import-ant and rewarding joint venture: four remarkable children, Chase, Andrew, Lara, and Hanna. I am grateful for their support. Together we enjoy a wonderful life. At some point, even our children took up the cadence of "how's the book?" I promise the next one will not require the same pestering.

ABOUT THE AUTHOR

Todd Zenger is a global expert on topics of corporate strategy, strategic leadership, and organization design. He has lectured widely on these topics to audiences at most of the world's leading business schools and has published extensively in the leading academic journals on management and strategy. Zenger is the newly appointed N. Eldon Tanner Chair in Strategy and Strategic Leadership at the David Eccles School of Business at the University of Utah. He also holds the designation of Presidential Professor at the University of Utah and is chair of the Entrepreneurship and Strategy department. From 1990 to 2014, he served on the faculty of Washington University's Olin Business School, where he was the long-standing chair of the strategy group and academic director of the executive MBA program. Zenger completed his undergraduate degree in economics at Stanford University and his PhD in strategy and organization at UCLA. Zenger is active in consulting and executive teaching in the areas of strategy and strategic leadership. He writes for the *Harvard Business Review* on topics of strategy.

www.toddzenger.com
@toddzenger